For Laura, Maximillian & Mabel
Thanks for putting up with my obsession.

To David 'da' Lyons, you lived life to the full.
You were fearless, brave, bright and brilliant!
Love and miss you bruv.

THE PROCESS

Copyright © James Bowden, 2016

James Bowden is hereby identified as author of this work in accordance with Section 77 of the Copyright, Designs and Patents Act 1988

All rights reserved, including the right to reproduce this book, or portions thereof in any form.
No part of this text may be reproduced, transmitted, downloaded, decompiled, reverse engineered, or stored, in any form or introduced into any information storage and retrieval system, in any form or by any means, whether electronic or mechanical without the express written permission of the author.

ISBN-10: 1535182687
ISBN-13: 978-1535182683

CONTENTS

PART 1

Chapter 1	About this book	1
Chapter 2	Inspiration	5
Chapter 3	What is The Process?	8
Chapter 4	Imagination	14
Chapter 5	The State of Being	23
Chapter 6	Instinct	26
Chapter 7	Believe (BE/ LEAVE)	34
Chapter 8	Truth	39
Chapter 9	It all comes from you!	43
Chapter 10	We all learn differently	51
Chapter 11	The power of words	53
Chapter 12	The power of the mind	56

PART 2

The Head

Chapter 13	The Head	62

The Heart

Chapter 14	The Heart	80
Chapter 15	Work from the heart not the brain	96
Chapter 16	Internalisation	101

The Body

Chapter 17	The Body	108
Chapter 18	Physicalisation	113
Chapter 19	The Next Steps	127

About the author

James graduated from Rose Bruford in 1994 and has worked regularly as an actor in Theatre and TV. His career has been diverse, appearing in the original West End cast of 'The Beautiful Game', open air Shakespeare, pantomime, repertory theatre, off West End, number one tours, TV and music videos. James has also trained as a teacher for both adults and secondary school students. He also teaches The Process to professional actors at The Actor's Centre, London. In 2007 he started The Dorset School of Acting with his wife Laura Roxburgh and has trained countless young people in acting and performance, developing their performance skills in acting, singing and dancing. In 2011 DSA launched a one year diploma course in Acting and Musical Theatre where James developed The Process, a fundamental element of the training at The Dorset School of Acting. This approach has proven to be extremely successful, with his students gaining places in employment, Vocational Drama Schools and also with actors' agencies.

James lives by the sea in Dorset and also teaches The Process both in London and internationally.

Acknowledgements

There are a number of people I would like to thank for all their help and support over the last few years as I have been putting my ideas together and creating this book. They all believed in me enough to help push me to create The Process and believe in myself enough to finally put finger to keyboard and crystallise my ideas. Firstly I have to thank my wife Laura Roxburgh without whose help The Process would never have been possible. It was whilst trying to help her with a particular acting challenge that I stumbled upon the secret of truthful acting. Thanks to Susie Burdekin; your advice and knowledge have been integral for me to be able to capture all of The Process and finally solidify my ideas into print. Mel Churcher; thanks for supporting The Dorset School of Acting and allowing me to shadow you and realise that I have the ability to be an acting coach and develop my own approach to acting. John Gillet; thanks for inspiring me to write down my ideas, your direction and advice have been invaluable throughout my career. I would also like to thank Nicola Bowden for her tireless commitment to making this book look right and Susan Elkin for her feedback and honesty, which has shaped the finished book. Thanks also to my copy editor Elizabeth Parks for making sure that what I have written makes sense. I also have to thank all of those that have gone before and whose work has influenced and inspired me on my journey to creating The Process. I may not have agreed with all of your ideas, but where we have diverged The Process has emerged. Finally I would like to thank my family for all their support and tolerance while I obsessed over this book and The Process.

THE PROCESS
the secret of truthful acting

There is no one system or method that can be held to be the only way to approach creating a character. There are many different stimuli which affect different people in different ways. Always remember that the tool-kit offered here has many different tools and not all of them are appropriate to use every time. You wouldn't use a hammer to remove a nut when a spanner is the perfect tool for the job! Take and use what you need, what helps you discover the truth and create real emotions and physical lives for your characters. Remember any system or method is primarily for the rehearsal room, there are a couple of elements that are essential for the screen or stage, but none of the techniques outlined in this book should be dwelt upon once you start to perform the role.

The key thing to remember is that on screen or stage an actor has enough to contend with so always: Keep It Simple, Stupid.

Chapter 1
About this book

"Two roads diverged in a wood and I -
I took the one less traveled by."
                                        Robert Frost

N.A.R.
In the late 90's I had the good fortune, whilst on an open air Shakespeare tour across the UK, to work with a very wise actor who had a great deal of experience. He noticed in me the zealous drive for perfection and desire for art that at times infected the work I did if I felt that things were not up to scratch. I would become very angry and upset if I didn't hit it in every performance or if other cast members didn't take their work seriously. This actor, Frank Jarvis, had been acting for decades and had worked with Sir Michael Caine in 'The Italian Job' amongst others so had gleaned a great deal of knowledge over his long career. He took me aside and reminded me that at the end of the day what we were doing was creating popcorn and candyfloss for the audience, in other words, entertaining them. Some would discover the deeper meaning in what we did but if the audience were entertained we had achieved our primary aim. He also told me of an experience he had whilst working with the actor Richard Widmark. Widmark had taken Frank aside whilst working on a series called 'Madigan' and told him of a time he worked with Cary Grant. Widmark had noticed that on Grant's script he had written the initials N.A.R on certain shots. Widmark asked him what it meant and Grant replied that those shots were when he was out of frame and therefore he was reminding himself that there was No Acting Required!

Now, this phrase has stuck in my mind all these years and although in a very different context, it has become a vital acronym when looking at the art and craft of acting. The biggest mistake actors make when performing is to 'act'. Acting is fake, it is putting something on, it is lying to the audience. All performers should feel the truth and just be when they are in front of the camera or on the stage. The secret to this truth is to stop 'acting' and just be. Keep the acronym N.A.R. in the forefront of your mind when you are preparing to perform and you will be able to access the most important element of the actor's art and craft, The Truth! Whether you are an experienced actor or have just started your journey toward a career as a professional actor, this book is for you. Over the next chapters you will discover a series of ideas and exercises that will help you to become a brilliant and truthful actor.

Why do you need The Process? What use is it to you? Well, if you are a seasoned professional you will know what it is like to really hit the role, but you will also have experienced those painful moments when it felt as if your inspiration deserted you. This book will give you the tools to create truthful, believable and real characters consistently. If you are new to acting you will find the tools an essential way to take a character from the pages of a script into reality. If you follow the suggestions every time you approach a role, I guarantee you will feel a difference. The Process is the secret of truthful acting, and you have just discovered it, so use it well.

As you read this book you will notice that it is broken into two parts. Part 1 is the what, it outlines the key ideas of The Process, it explains what you need to have in order to create real and truthful emotions and what you need to do to be a truly real and believable performer. Part 2 is the how, it gives you the practical tools that will enable you to master your emotions in performance and create truth whilst you perform. It illustrates the practical application of The Process and gives you a clear and direct route to creating a real living, breathing character. It is separated into three different areas, Mind, Heart and Body. These represent the three different steps in character creation. First, as an actor you must use your Mind to analyse the script, break it down, make it make sense and tease out all the clues the writer has hidden in its depths which give life to the words on the page. Next the actor must work from the Heart in order to create the truth and inner life of the character. Finally the actor must use the Body to inhabit a believable physicality and so finally create a truly rounded human being from the words of the writer.

If you follow The Process you will find that your performance will be more truthful and believable and most importantly, consistent. The Process is the only way to guarantee that your performance will be truly brilliant.

JAMES BOWDEN

PART 1

Chapter 2
Inspiration

*"Inspiration is hard to come by.
You have to take it where you find it."*
Bob Dylan

Inspiration is what every actor is searching for when they perform. It is ethereal and as intangible as fog. It is the adrenaline rush you feel when you know everything is right. It is when you are as close to the life and world of your character as you can be. It is the addictive quality of performance. Ask any actor what drives them to perform and they will tell you that it is when they are *being* the character. This is only possible when they have been performing under the influence of inspiration. It is the Aha moment when you are flying and experiencing that moment of oneness. It is when you know you have performed in the most truthful, believable way possible and both you and the audience know it. When you truly reach inspiration, you can feel it through your body. Your adrenaline levels rise but you are in complete control. It is very much like the sensation you feel when you enter fight or flight mode. You body is reacting physiologically to the mental state you are in and is preparing for action. It is this sensation that has a narcotic effect for most actors and is what they crave when they perform. Inspiration is the result of a performer reacting to truthful emotion and this only happens once they have entered into The State of Being.

There is a well-known anecdote about Sir Laurence Olivier after he had given what was arguably his best performance of Shakespeare's 'King Lear'. Apparently he ran from the stage as soon as the curtain dropped and locked himself away in his dressing room. He refused to respond or open the door for some time and was beside himself with frustration. When he finally let someone in they asked what was the matter and why he was so upset, as it was the best performance he had ever given. Olivier is reported to have replied, "I know! But I don't know how I did it!!!" He had been performing with inspiration but had no way of knowing how to replicate it. A lot of actors have some instinct and natural ability but don't know how they do it and they are not consistent.

It is exactly this reason, the lack of understanding how a performer managed to gain inspiration on screen or stage that has been the basis of a systematic approach to the art and craft of acting. It is why we use conscious exercises to affect the subconscious and it is the basis of the The Process.

THE PROCESS

THE STATE OF BEING

PERSONALISATION
REPLACEMENT
VISUALISATION
REALISATION
IMAGINATION

INSPIRATION

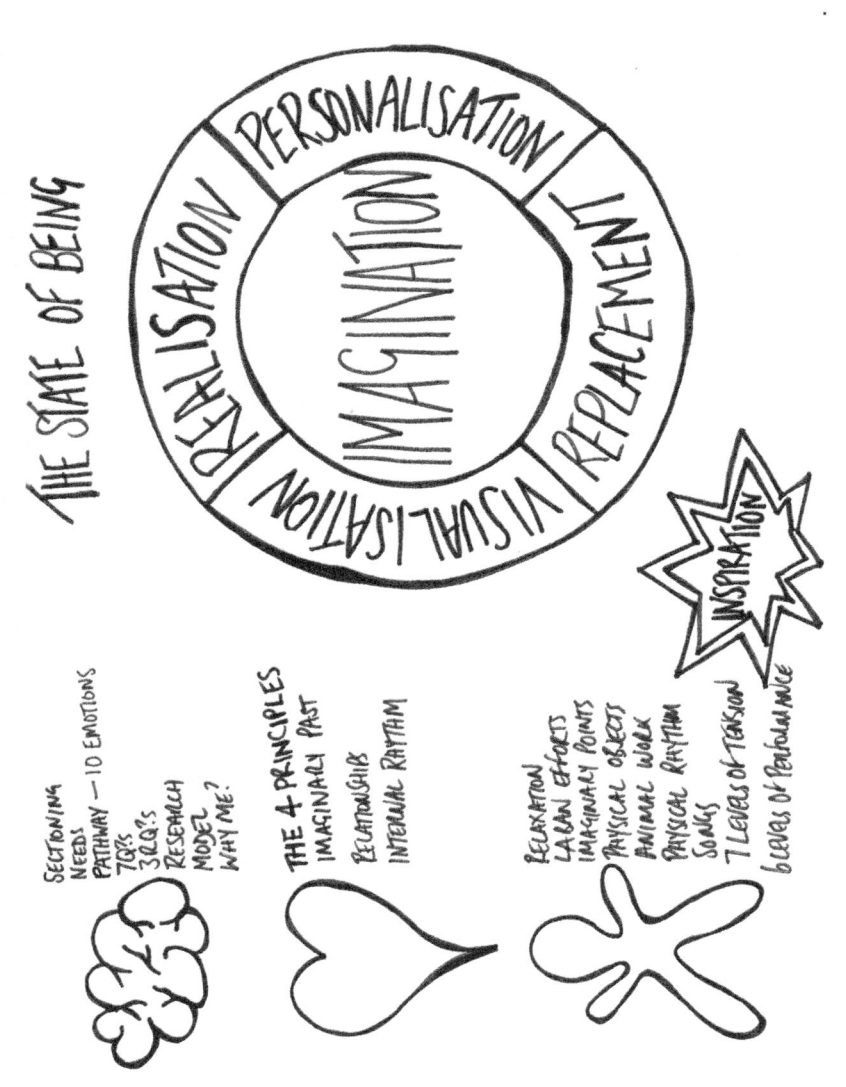

SECTIONING
NEEDS
PATHWAY — 10 EMOTIONS
7Q?S
3LQ?S
RESEARCH
MODEL
WHY ME?

THE 4-PRINCIPLES
IMAGINARY PAST
RELATIONSHIPS
INTERNAL RHYTHM

RELAXATION
LABAN EFFORTS
IMAGINARY POINTS
PHYSICAL OBJECTS
ANIMAL WALK
PHYSICAL RHYTHM
SOAKS
7 LEVELS OF TENSION
6 LEVELS OF PERFORMANCE

fig. 1

Chapter 3
What is The Process?

"If you can't describe what you are doing as a process, you don't know what you're doing"
W. Edwards Deming

The Process is the secret of truthful acting! It is a systematic approach to acting that guarantees truthful emotions and a full connection to the life and world of a character. If you approach the exercises in this book with an open mind and really put into practice the concepts, you will become a more consistent and truthful performer. It is the touch paper to true creativity and helps to create the spark of truth in every performance.

You will have heard of many different systems of acting and know of a few high profile actors who have a preferred method of getting into character. These range from the old school like Laurence Olivier whose adage was, "Try acting, it's much easier" and who believed in, "Saying your lines and not bumping into the furniture", to Daniel Day Lewis whose approach is total immersion in the character which results in him being in character for the length of the shoot. The Process is my take on a number of different approaches and systems, from Stanislavski's original 'System' to the Group Theatre's three key teachers' (Adler, Meisner and Strasberg) methodologies, together with a large measure of my own discoveries of how to create truth.

The problem with all these methodologies is that they are so involved and convoluted it is easy to become tangled up and confused and not know what the hell you are supposed to be doing. Stanislavski is arguably the Godfather of Naturalistic acting; his 'System' was a continual work in progress and he was still adding and taking away exercises and concepts till his death. The result was a myriad of exercises that he developed and overlapped and by its very size it became unwieldy and in some parts confusing. His 'System' had two key elements: 'Internal Training' and 'External Training'. After Stanislavski, other notable pioneers of a systematical approach to acting developed the concepts from his work with different central foci. These included Lee Strasberg, the creator of 'The Method' who took the internal aspect of Stanislavski's 'System' and developed it further. Sanford Meisner focused more on developing the actor's instinct by getting his actors to really listen and react to the other performer on stage. Stella Adler, who upholds that she was the first American to work with Stanislavski in person, focused on the actor's actions and what and how these actions are done on stage or screen. There are many more approaches to creating character that are too multifarious to mention but suffice it to say there is a need for a simple approach that can help you find your way through the minefield as you develop your skills as an actor.

The Process is a streamlined systematic approach to acting that takes elements of other methodologies, distills them, simplifies them and uses them with a strong focus on the actor's imagination. The main idea is to focus on the key elements that work in order to free up the actor's mind so he or she can stop thinking when performing and just be. The core elements of The Process create truth in the actor whilst the other elements help create a more in-depth characterisation. Meisner believed that the character came from their actions in the script and what they say. I believe that it is more than this and that an actor must also create a real physical life for the character.

The Process is a crucial element in performing: it allows the actor to create truth, it gives the actor an approach to the role and it ensures that all the performances are consistent. It is the route to inspiration. Inspiration is ethereal, impossible to pin down so you need a conscious system to coax it out of you. The key aim of The Process is to use conscious methods to affect the sub-conscious, which is where truth resides. If you convince your sub-conscious that you are feeling an emotion you will start to feel it truthfully. The problem is that inspiration cannot be accessed at will and it is only through this manipulation of the sub-conscious that you are able to trick it to release real emotions. So by using conscious exercises you can make your sub-conscious respond to and gain inspiration. I use The Four Principles to consciously manipulate the actor's sub-conscious.

The Process is a three-pronged system to go from page to stage, it is an approach that provides a set of tools to create truth. The actor starts with the Mind when beginning to work with the text, this is the starting point for the character. There is a set of exercises that you will discover later, to help you tame the text and make it work for you. The second element of The Process uses the Heart, this is Internalisation, this is the essence of the character and at the centre of this aspect is the core of The Process, the imagination. The exercises that use the imagination are The Four Principles, which are Realisation, Visualisation, Personalisation and Replacement but more of these later. The third element is the Body, which involves the Physicalisation of the character. This is the final layer of the character and is the external life, the one that the world sees.

THE PROCESS

Once the internal truth has been created you can use the external exercises to create a complete character.

When you perform, you will find or have found times when everything is working and you are flying with the character, you are firing on all cylinders but conversely there are times when you don't feel it and you are not in the role. The point of The Process is that it helps you to be consistent. By having a conscious means of creating character you know that you will always produce the goods. A key thing about having a systematic approach to character is that you are no longer relying on fate to allow inspiration to hit. You are in control and can feel the role every time. If you know how to create a real emotional response from yourself you will always be truthful, and therefore be performing with inspiration.

The basis of The Process is using your imagination to its full potential. It is this that will help you create emotions truthfully. The only way to capitalise on your imagination is to imagine yourself in a set of circumstances that is personal to you and will elicit the emotional response that you need for the character. This is Realisation, the first of The Four Principles. Imagination is the creative juice, it is limitless and you can use it to create any emotion that you need. It is ridiculous to think that it is the most underused facility an actor has. Imagination is the one element that has been forgotten in the development of other methodologies. It is given a passing mention and then other exercises are used to try and elicit truth from the actor. A lot of time is spent on self-analysis and forcing emotions, imagination is the thing that actually can create truthful emotional responses in an actor.
The thing to remember about The Process is that it is not Stanislavski's 'System' or an iteration of 'The Method'. As I

have previously said, there are a many elements to Stanislavski's 'System' and so much actually changed during his life. There are over twenty volumes that exist in Russia of Stanislavski's actual work, in the West we only have four books so what is taught is really an edited version. Also, as Stanislavski was drawing to the end of his life, the focus of his 'System' was shifting from an internal and external approach to a predominantly external approach. He had decided that 'Emotion Memory' was no longer a viable way to create truth. However 'Emotion Memory' became a central part of character creation in 'The Method'. With the different versions of 'The Method' there is still a focus on the self-analytical approach to creating character; the need to actually experience situations and circumstances in order to reproduce them in performance. This focus on; "what if I were in this situation?" can create a barrier between the character and the actor. The Process changes the focus and brings the character to the actor. It forces the actor to use his or her imagination, as this is a renewable source. If you rely on 'Emotion Memory' to create an emotional response you are relying on something that is mutable. Your memories change over time as you get older and do not hold the same strength over you. For example, when I was eighteen I was mugged by the local thug and his gang whilst I was leaving school. This was a very traumatic experience, which resulted in a night at the accident and emergency department of the local hospital. For years I found this memory painful; it would throw me into a violent temper. This incident was too raw and I would mull it over and continue to relive the nightmare. It had a very negative impact on my life. If I were to use this memory to get a sense of anger and fear in my acting I would indeed have those feelings for the first few years, as it was an event that had had a profound impact on my young life. Now as I look at that event I don't feel the same, it does not have an effect on me at all so it would be no good to use if I needed to re-create that anger and fear I felt all those years ago. Memories have a half-life and decay with time. Moreover, considering we will not always have had appropriate memories to create the right emotion within us throughout our lives, we will have to find a different way to produce those emotions. The only thing we have at our disposal is our imagination, this is fertile and inexhaustive and, if used correctly, is very powerful.

Chapter 4
Imagination

*"Logic will get you from A to Z,
imagination will get you everywhere"*
                                    Albert Einstein

The imagination is at the heart of The Process. It is the most important element of creating truth and is the most powerful creative tool an actor has. Although it is mentioned in Stanislavski's work with 'If' and is the lever into his creative state, it is something that is often overlooked. It is something that we all take for granted - of course an actor uses their imagination, but the key thing is how they use it. Meisner introduced the idea of using the imagination but his focus on instinct and reacting and repetition eclipses its importance. The imagination is the forgotten element of our art and craft. Its importance is over shadowed in 'The Method's' use of 'Emotion Memory' and certain method actors need to be continually in character whilst on set between takes (this is a good thing to do but the correct use of your imagination is paramount). Imagination is the gateway to the truth, it is only through using it effectively that you can really convince your sub-conscious to release your inspiration. It links most of the elements of The Process together; if you do not use your imagination effectively you will not be able to go through Realisation, you wont be able to Personalise, you won't be able to Visualise and it will be impossible to use Replacement. It will be impossible to get into The State of Being, you will not be able to believe, you will have no truth and you will find your performance hollow and lacking life. The benefit of imagination is that it is boundless and limitless, it never runs out and it can always be fresh unlike memories.

A key thing to remember is that when you were a young child, you were constantly using your imagination but as you grew up it was suppressed. Do you remember being told to grow up and to act your age? You are actors so you should never grow up - if I acted my age I would go mad, I'd be considered middle aged...no way!!! People used to say, "He has a very fertile imagination" as if it were a bad thing. You really need to embrace your inner child and let your imagination run riot. Just take a moment to remember the crazy scenarios you used to create as a kid to entertain yourself, the monsters that lurked in a wardrobe or under your bed when the lights went out. The key thing to remember is that you really used to believe in those monsters, enough to scream at night for your parents to come and save you. The biggest problem with our lives today is that we just don't have the time to play anymore, in life, in performance, in rehearsal. You really now have to take the responsibility to exercise your imagination. Like anything else it is a muscle that will get flabby and weak if it's not used so it is important to use conscious exercises to allow your sub-conscious free rein.

EXERCISES

Day Dream This is the easiest way to use and develop your imagination. Imagine winning the lotto. What would you spend your money on? Really go to town, who would you give money to? Who wouldn't you give your money to? What house would you have? What luxuries would you buy? Really believe your new life. Be specific. Imagine what it would be like to right a wrong that you have not been able to in the past. Maybe an insult or an event you never righted. Live out your imagined responses - these are fuelled by your subconscious.

Cloud Watching The game you used to play as a child. Lie down in a field, garden or park and watch the clouds. Start to see the shapes in them, a dinosaur, a unicorn, a rabbit, a car and so on. Challenge yourself to see the most bizarre items and imagine them coming to life. What voice do they have? What characteristics? Be as creative as you can.

Blind Tourist A trust and imagination game.
Get into pairs and select one person as A and the other as B. B will be blindfolded and A will be the tour guide. A will take B's arm and guide them through an imaginary city, whispering in their ear and telling them about the fantastical sights. A needs to be very specific and paint a very vivid image of the world in which they are in. This will exercise the imagination of both the tour guide and tourist. After a few minutes B has the blindfold removed and both guide and tourist discuss favourite elements or areas of the imagined city. The process is then reversed so A becomes the tourist and B the guide.

Tall Tales (in other words, over embellished Story Telling.) Also know as Baron Munchausen. The group sit in a circle and one person tells the most imaginative over embellished story that they can with the most absurd ending. Each person in the group then has an opportunity to tell their tale trying to out-do their predecessor. A development of this exercise is that the first person starts the story and then after a few minutes the next person develops it as much as they can. The story then continues around the group until it reaches the first person who finishes the story in the most absurd manner.

Imaginative Play In a space, start to imagine playing like a child with an imaginative world individually. Create your own world, play with imaginary toys, create imaginative scenarios, create a fort with items in the room. Really commit to that childlike quality that we all used to have when we were younger. As you become engrossed in the world you have created, start to invite the other kids in the room to play. Just be in the moment, don't block ideas and have fun!!!

There is one thing to be aware of when using imagination in your acting. It is not merely a matter of just imagining that the weapon you are holding is loaded, you have to use really compelling and strong scenarios to affect your emotions and engage them fully. You need to picture your imagination process like an enormous funnel that you can topload with images and vignettes the bigger the imagined scenario the more useful they will be (see fig.2). Now picture trying to squeeze the images into the funnel and as you press, ever so slowly you can see a drop forming on the thin end of the funnel. This is the amount of truthful emotion you are getting out of the imaginative scenarios you are creating.

fig.2

THE PROCESS

You need to draw the character to you as this is the only way to be truthful, so use your life experience in the Imaginary Circumstances you create and make this scenario echo the character's circumstances. This is not the same as Stanislavski's 'If' which says, 'What if I were in this situation?'. The distinction is you change the question to, 'What imaginary situation would make me feel like this?'. It is a subtle difference, but as you will find when we discuss Realisation, it is a vital one. This will elicit a truthful response to the circumstances your character is in. Imagination is the vital step in helping you to get into a state of being.

When working with your imagination you really need to ensure that you push the boundaries. It is essential that you take risks with yourself and be brave otherwise you will not create enough emotional stimulus and your attempts to work with your imagination will be pointless as they will not affect you. Another key mistake actors make is to create a really compelling Imaginary Circumstance and then be surprised when they have a truthful response to it and immediately suppress the emotion. Be brave. Let it happen, let the emotion take control and see how far it will go. All this is done in the rehearsal room or on your own initially until you find out what really works for you and how strong the emotion is. It's worth noting that humans are needlessly superstitious and are worried that if they imagine a scenario which involves those close to them, somehow that scenario will actually happen in real life. It won't, all that will happen if you worry about jinxing your loved ones is that your performance will be affected. You will be too scared to imagine the unimaginable and so will imagine a half hearted, pointless scenario that won't produce even an ounce of truthful emotion. One scenario I use as an example is if I wanted to feel the most compelling form of guilt I would imagine a scenario where I reverse my car out of the drive and knock down and kill my seven year old daughter. That is a compelling imaginary scenario that will really affect me and produce a real emotional reaction. Once a female student was unsure what would she need to imagine to feel totally destroyed inside. I said, "You can imagine what it would be like to be raped can't you?" Initially she responded in the typical way saying she couldn't imagine what that would be like, but what she was actually saying that she didn't want to imagine what that was like. She was scared of doing what it takes to get a real emotional response. Of course she could imagine what it was like to be raped, and if she invested in that horrific imaginary scenario fully, there is no doubt that it would have produced a very strong and believable emotional response. The important thing to remember is that it is just your imagination and you cannot conjure the bogeyman just by imagining it! I remember watching a movie once called 'Candyman' when I was younger. It was an urban legend about a murderous spirit called Candyman who would appear if you looked into a mirror and called out his name five times. He would then kill the summoner with his hooked hand. It had a profound effect on my superstitious brother and myself and needless to say for years I would never tempt fate by calling out 'Candyman' in front of a mirror. We did toy with saying it once or twice but we got spooked and didn't dare to continue. This demonstrates the power of superstition regardless of how ridiculous those superstitions may be! Ironically it also shows the power of your imagination when you let it master you. Don't let yourself block your imagination pointlessly, really be brave and you will coax tremendous and powerfully true emotions in your performance.

THE PROCESS

Another thing to remember about your imagination is that it can always be fresh. It doesn't get old or stale like memories. When you are on a long run in a show it is inevitable that you are going to find it hard to reproduce the same emotion eight times a week or take after take on a film set. It will start to get stale after a while and you need to have a different stimulus to help you regain that creativity and the honesty of your performance. Imagination never runs out! You have at your fingertips a limitless creative fuel that will always help you when you need it. It will not fade or dry up. You just need to exercise it and really push your boundaries so you will have a fantastic resource that can always be used. You have an imagination otherwise you would not be embarking on, or have embarked on, this mad career. You don't need to stay up for seventy eight hours just because that's what the character is supposed to do in the script. You have been tired before, how do you feel emotionally if you have stayed up for so long? Angry? Fearful? Sad? There is no need to focus on the physical state. You don't need to get friends to imprison you and beat you regularly so that you know what it is like to be an abused prisoner. You need to use your imagination and that will give you all the emotional truth that you need.

EXERCISE

Observe a person Observe someone in the high street or park or shopping centre. Imagine their life, what they are doing and why they are doing it. What has happened to them up to this point? What are they going to do? Create a rich imaginative set of circumstances for them, the more fantastical the better.

Re-create an activity without props Initially with props, complete an action (for example, setting a table, preparing a meal.) Once you have completed the action remove the props and repeat the action with as much detail as possible. Really see the items you used, create it truthfully and be specific!

Rorschach Inkblots
Look at the inkblots in a group, all call out what you see in each inkblot and then see what else you can see. Let your mind open and react on instinct. Next try and develop your ideas, make the images more and more fantastical. Really push your imagination.

Chapter 5
The State of Being

"In the creative state a man is taken out of himself. He lets down as it were a bucket into his subconscious, and draws up something which is normally beyond his reach. He mixes this thing with his normal experiences and out of the mixture he makes a work of art."

E M Forster

The State of Being is the creative state that you need to be in before you are able to perform truthfully. It is where inspiration lies. It is the state that you are attempting to place yourself in before you engage with anything on screen or stage. Once you are in this state everything is in place for inspiration to hit. All the exercises that you will use prior to performing will all converge into this state. The idea is to use all of these conscious exercises to place yourself in the State of Being. Then you are ready to perform. It is the State of Being that enables you to access your inspiration and sustain truthful emotions throughout your performance. Once in The State of Being you experience that sense of flying or the Aha moment when everything clicks into place and you truly hit it.

It is essential to start from The State of Being in order to allow your emotions freedom to express themselves. Like a roller coaster, you need to be at the top of the ride to allow the rest of the journey to happen. This is a simplified version of the 'Overall Creative State' that Stanislavski was attempting to create with his 'System'. The key difference is that this state is achieved psychologically whereas the physical side of The

Process is produced more instinctively. Stanislavski wanted his actors to attain a creative state both psychologically and physically. I feel that the problem with this is that it really starts to complicate The Process and confuse an actor. Remember the point of The Process is to give actors the tools without cluttering up their head!

It is crucial to be in The State of Being on screen or stage. If you are not in the state, you are not in the right frame of mind or operating in the zone. You will not be able to access your emotions truthfully and will start to 'act'. We will make this distinction later when we look at the importance of the words that we use. It is only if you are in The State of Being that you can allow your instinct to fully take over. Once you have attained this state you will find that you can react, give, perform, feel truthfully and your performance will move from the realm of good to true brilliance. The Four Principles are designed to aid this process.

A key thing to take on board now is that this perfect state can only be attained once you have completed all of the exercises and techniques in rehearsal and then put it all to the back of your mind and forgotten everything. Actors spend too much time analysing everything and do not allow their performances to be ruled by their heart, which is vital as you will read later on in this book. Once you have completed the Mind or analytical elements of The Process you must stop using your head and allow your heart to drive your performance. You need to stop thinking and trust in your instincts. All the conscious work you do is for the rehearsal and preparation element of your craft. Once you have completed this and are performing, you are then engaging in the Art element. Stanislavski commented that an actor should, "Work on the

System at home. On stage put it to one side". This is just as true for any system that an actor may use; if you think too much you will get in the way of your performance and block your truthful responses. Only when you allow your subconscious free rein in your performance can you really create art.

All of the exercises and core principles that you will work on in The Process are designed to put you in this state so that you can perform truthfully with real emotions. It is only by following the central principles that you will prepare your conscious mind to allow your subconscious mind take over and release your instinct.

Chapter 6
Instinct

"Acting is just a process of relaxation, actually. Knowing the text so well and trusting that the instinct and the subconscious mind, whatever you want to call it, is going to take over."
Anthony Hopkins

Instinct as an actor is absolutely essential. We are instinctive creatures, we often feel emotion from the gut. Humans are instinctive creatures and often feel emotion in any given situation. We have an instant reaction to people we meet, what they say, how they behave. Therefore we must allow our instinct free rein on the screen or stage. How many times have you met someone whom you instantly like or dislike? Instinct is what drives us as humans to make choices and the characters we create must also be driven by this.

As an actor you must always act on your instincts. So often in rehearsals I see actors suppress a move. You can see them attempt to move but then they think better of it for no apparent reason other than they are afraid of committing to their own instincts. If it goes against the director's wishes, they will tell you, but invariably a good director will see that you were working from instinct and it will work. The key rule in instinct is 'if you feel it…do it!'. It is so important that you follow this maxim. It is this that makes your performance real. Often you can see actors shadow movements whilst performing, these are gestures, glances, movements that their body is trying to do but the intellect of the actor is not allowing them to be realised.

THE PROCESS

There may be a time that your instinct to move doesn't fit within the context of the scene that you are working on, but at least you listened to yourself. The more you allow it to operate the more often you will feel instinctive moments in your performance.

You need to bring your own instincts to the rehearsal to create real life. If you do not, then you are not being a complete actor, you are not bringing to the creative process the full package. It is also very important that even after the rehearsal process you use your instinct in performance. This is what keeps your role or character alive. You may get some resistance from less enlightened cast members who have been trained in a very fixed way but eventually they will revel in the truth of your performance and will allow your instinctive changes to affect them and their performances, thus keeping the performance alive. Goldie Hawn commented on working with Meryl Streep saying that no one take whilst filming was the same. This is because Meryl Streep is constantly working from her instinct and adapting to all the different nuances that are being given to her from her fellow actors. You should strive to be that kind of performer!

CASE STUDY

Whilst working with one of my students on Hamlet's speech in Act 1 Scene 2 where he is wishing that his body would just evaporate or that he could commit suicide as the world that God had created was of no worth, the student's shadow movement betrayed the false emotion that he was trying to use. When Hamlet finally challenges God, the actor's instinct was to look up at the source of his anguish. I saw the actor lift his head and glance briefly upwards instinctively but almost as quickly, he forced his eyeline and head down and looked towards the ground into the middle distance. His shadow movements betrayed his instincts. I could see that he felt the need to challenge God but for some reason he suppressed his instinct. I stopped him and asked him whether he had realised what he had done - because he had been working so hard trying to feel the emotion of the scene, he had totally ignored his instinct. Be aware, your body can betray you and show an audience what you really should be doing. Pay attention!

Many actors get so worried about getting it right that they fail to follow their instinct. Just because a director tells you to do something, doesn't necessarily mean it is truthful. We are performing in a world that is intrinsically false. We have to do our best as creative beings to make it truthful. A director can only put forward his or her ideas and then employ actors to bring their creative faculties to make those ideas real and alive. It is your job to use your instinct fully to make this happen. Being right is good but bringing your instinct to the game and being raw is better. It is more vibrant and exciting to watch. How many times have you seen a performance that is so riveting, truthful and exciting that has inspired and uplifted you? These performances are rooted in the actor's instinct. How many times have you seen a technically strong performance that has left you cold? You can see that it has been well executed but there is a reason why you have not been affected. This is because the performer is not operating with his or her instinct. These actors have either been trained to get everything perfect at the expense of truth. Or they have just picked up this bad habit.

THE PROCESS

CASE STUDY

A group of West End producers created a consortium to offer West End shows to a cruise liner. This kind of show had not been tried on the ships before as the normal entertainment had consisted of dance-heavy revue shows with strong singers. It was the first time that shows that were script reliant were being presented to the audience. Because of this, the consortium had to employ performers with acting experience as well as singing and dancing experience - musical theatre performers! As this venture was for two different ships the producers needed two casts to rehearse the same shows.
It was interesting to see the different nature of the two casts. One team consisted of performers who were very strong in getting the moves exactly as they were directed; the notes were perfect, the words were always right. This was the blue team. The other team, the red team, were much more raw, they played on stage, performers would sometimes be in a slightly different place than in rehearsals. The dances were always tight and the songs always contained the right notes but there seemed to be something different with their show. It really engaged the audience in a different way. Don't get me wrong, the blue team's shows were excellent, but they seemed to lack something in comparison. The difference was that the 'raw' red team were operating on instinct so their shows had more soul and affected the audiences more.
An audience can feel the difference between mechanical excellence and a raw instinctive performance. Be that kind of performer!

So you realise the importance of instinct but how do you develop it? One key practitioner whose main focus is instinct is Sanford Meisner. Originally one of the members of the influential Group Theatre which also consisted of Stella Adler and Lee Strasberg, Meisner decided that the key element an actor needed to develop was their instinct and to stop them 'acting' but rather to become reactive and so developed exercises to do this.

Meisner - Repetition Exercises
Designed to develop the actor's listening, and their ability to react to their partner, Meisner asked his students to observe something in their partner and comment on it, "That's a nice pink shirt", exactly. This a form of 're-booting' the actor so that they stop working on habit but get to a point where they can really listen to their partner. The exercise develops to a point where the observer makes a comment that is not true, "Where did you get those black boots?" (where the partner is wearing flip flops) and through the repetition the partner instinctively has no choice but to correct the question,"These are not black boots, they are red flip flops!". The key point is to only make the change when you feel the instinct to do so after really listening to your partner.

According to William Esper, a student of Meisner and later a teacher of Meisner's methods, the changes in the repetition come out of four conditions:

- Honest impulse - making the statement true. Keeping your response honest.
- Pile up - a response from frustration of an inaccurate observation.
- Express your opinion - responding truthfully with your point of view
- Responding to your partner's behaviour - If they walk away from you or respond to your statement or question with silence.

THE PROCESS

All of these conditions are affected by instinct and by doing these exercises you will develop your instinctive response to any given situation.

Esper says that the reasons we use Meisner's repetition exercises when developing our skill are:
- It takes an actor out of their head and makes them work from the heart.
- It forces an actor to listen.
- It forces the actor to really respond.
- It forces the actor to work moment to moment.
- It forces the actor into real spontaneity.

The repetition exercises are developed to 'The knock at the door' where the actors improvise a scene where one actor is in a room engaged in an independent activity[1] and the other actor knocks on the door to gain entrance. After knocking three times (responding to their own knock or lack of admittance each time) they enter and engage in the repetition exercise. This becomes an improvised scene where the actor engaged in the activity is so involved in it and the other actor is intent on continuing to talk. This conflict should result in both actors responding to each other and the situation instinctively and creating a small watchable scene. This exercise develops to include the entering actor entering with a purpose or objective. It teaches the actors to improvise using their instinct, which is vital for the following exercise.

---

[1] an exercise where the actor engages in an activity that takes up their complete attention . (See The Actor's Art and Craft: William Esper Teaches the Meisner Technique - Anchor Books)

Meisner & Esper - Criminal Action Problems

This exercise is an excellent way to truly develop your instinct as an actor. This should only be attempted once you have mastered the 'Knock at the door' with independent activity exercises.

The basis of this exercise is that one actor is creeping into the room to commit a crime. The partner can either be in the room asleep or about to enter imminently. This creates a sense of urgency and heightens the instinct of the actors.

The actor entering must come in the room with an objective. They must create a circumstance that means it is absolutely essential to enter the room to commit a crime. For example the person entering needs to get to the partner's phone to remove a text that they have accidentally sent to them that was meant for their secret lover. Or they want to steal money or an object of value for a very motivating reason. There has to be a real sense of consequence if they are caught in order to up the stakes. This exercise is undertaken without talking during the criminal action but if they are caught the actors can improvise. The actor entering the space is responsible for creating the circumstance, they are responsible for any specific props that are required and they must create the reasons for the following:

1. What do I need? To steal or change?
2. Why do I need it? Why do I have to commit this crime?
3. Where is the thing that I need located? It should be a place where you are not supposed to be.
4. When is it? When is the best time for the crime to take place? At night when they are asleep? Early in the morning when they are not there?
5. Who are they? What is the relationship with the other person? (remember - even total strangers is a relationship)

You can vary the location and circumstances, make it as challenging as you want. The actor with the objective should choose an activity that means they will be there as long as possible meaning the chance of getting caught is greater. The victim doesn't have to start in the room, they may return or check in from time to time. There can be more than one person in the room to begin with, for example a couple in bed asleep. If the actor entering is fully engaged, their adrenalin will be really pumping and they will be acting instinctively to every creak or response from the victim.

Imaginary Crisis Improvisation A group exercise that really develops your listening and responding skills as well as your instinct as an actor.

Create a circumstance that has a real sense of danger for the whole group. For example, you are trapped in a room after an earthquake, you are stranded on a deserted island, a plane has just crashed into your place of work or you are waking up after a crash. Each actor needs to decide independently who they are and the reason they are in that location, and also an objective (for example, they are there for an appointment, they are a perpetrator of the crisis and so on.) The key thing in the improvisation is to start from the moment after the disaster has happened and all the actors are regaining consciousness. Throughout the improvisation the actors should respond to each other whilst keeping their own objective in mind. The idea is to develop the situation and find a solution for the crisis. Ensure that you adapt to the situations that are presented and don't decide on one course of action and bully your way to achieve your own objective. The aim is to use give and take and to find a solution as a group. Another version of this exercise is to have someone as an observer who can throw suggestions into the improvisation if it starts to stagnate.

Chapter 7
Believe (BE / LEAVE)

"I believe acting truly is harnessing the power of belief"
Heath Ledger

This is the only path to truth. Remember that truth is our ultimate goal as performers and you need to believe if you are going to create truth on the screen or stage. You not only have to believe in your own abilities as a performer, you need to have total and utter belief in the given and Imaginary Circumstances of the character. This is important as it is the only way that you will be able to coax your sub-conscious to release your inspiration. Without belief you cannot create truth.

Remember when you were young and you convinced yourself that something you imagined actually happened? As a child your imagination was limitless and you believed every scenario that you created with your whole being. Your toys could come to life and your pets would talk to you. You looked into the back of wardrobes expecting to find a path to Narnia! It is this absolute belief that you need to recapture if you want to be an emotionally truthful performer.

If you believe as a performer, the audience believes you. The great power that an actor has is to create an imaginary world on screen or stage and to draw the audience into that world and follow their story. You see this so many times when a great actor plies their trade. You buy into their imagined life completely. This happens because they believe in their Imaginary Circumstances completely.

THE PROCESS

When an actor believes, the audience actually feels their emotions. They can really empathise with the lives and actions of the characters they are watching and this in turn leads them to engage with the journey of a character.

As an audience you want to really connect with the characters and stories that you are watching and you want to experience a cathartic moment. It is that belief in the character's life that draws an audience to do this. When Jack dies in 'Titanic', when Val Jean dies in 'Les Misérables', when the audience witness the death of Sergeant Elias in 'Platoon' and when Albert is finally reunited with Joey in 'Warhorse', the audience experience the feelings of the characters involved and this is because the actors believe in their circumstances and in turn the audience believe in the characters.

If the actor doesn't believe in the character's experiences and world everything starts to disintegrate around them. They start to become aware of the false construct that is 'acting', they see the other actors on stage as people saying lines, they see the crew behind the camera and the magic all starts to disappear. The world that we create on the screen or stage is so fragile that if the actor stops believing we lose everything. Belief and truth are made of the most insubstantial and delicate material that they disintegrate as soon as they are touched. By touching I mean that you start to examine them and put them under scrutiny. As soon as you do this, be it with a lapse of concentration or by listening to that little critic inside your head, you will never be able to truly please. Everything will start to evaporate around you, the walls of artifice will start to fragment and reveal to you the false reality of an actor's world. As soon as everything starts to fall apart you become acutely aware of the charade and are unable to create truth. It is like trying to run up a sand dune, the harder you try the quicker the sand moves under your feet drawing you downwards. When this happens to an actor the result is catastrophic.

CASE STUDY
When I was second cover for a character in a West End show, I was foolish enough not to truly commit to my job. I knew that I would never actually get on to perform, as I was just an insurance policy for the insurance policy of the first cover. With this attitude pervading my work I never really learned my lines properly. This is not only very unprofessional but also very destructive. I was called for a rehearsal on stage by the associate director and was watched by the actor and first cover of the character I was covering. I started off fine, as I truly believed in the world I had created, but very quickly, as the lines started to desert me, it all started to crumble around me. I could no longer believe in the circumstances of the scene and became acutely aware of the audience and started to listen to the little voice in my head that was rightfully admonishing me for being so foolish and arrogant in not learning my lines properly. Finally I stood up, looked out front and called the first cover to take over and fled from the stage! I really lost my bottle, panicked and gave up. Things that an actor must never do. Thankfully it was just a rehearsal and not in front of a paying audience. If I had known my lines as I should have, I wouldn't have stopped believing and I wouldn't have felt so exposed. I would have been able to do what I was employed to do and just be.

After the actor becomes aware of the false reality and tries to fight back and start to 'act' the audience can see through them, see the fake truth and the actor will lose them too! In the end you have an actor labouring in vain trying to metaphorically grab the disappearing gossamer of their truth and an audience are left watching hollow, untruthful performances all because belief was lost.

Believe can be broken down into two key words that should be any actor's mantra:

BE - the actor must be present, there, in the moment reacting to what is happening there and then, not to a rehearsed reaction to something that has been in the rehearsal room. Actors must **BE**. You shouldn't 'act' or 'perform'. Nothing should be forced. You need to just **BE**! If you lose your way, you shouldn't struggle to force an emotion. If it is not there you can only go back to your imagination and believe in the circumstances to regain the truthful emotions and truth.

LEAVE - leave yourself alone! Let your instincts lead you. Trust in all the work you have done and believe in your ability. Once you perform you must **LEAVE** all the analytical technique in the rehearsal room. It is all well and good to have a system, but if you allow it to follow you into your performance it will clutter up your head and get in the way of you believing. So many times in the past I have had students who have rehearsed well but when we go for a run through they fall apart. They are not sure if they are coming or going because they start to worry about Stanislavski this or Stanislavski that and it leaves them dazed and confused. It is so important to just **BE** on screen or stage and just **LEAVE** yourself alone.

Belief is really one thing you cannot forget to use. This is the glue that makes The Four Principles effective and really fires your imagination. This in turn creates truthful emotions that then cement your belief in the world of the character.

Chapter 8
Truth

"Whatever satisfies the soul is truth"
                                    Walt Whittman

This is the ultimate goal of any actor. It is the holy grail and is what makes actors perform. This is what truly great actors want to achieve whilst performing. Truth can only be accessed through completely being in The State of Being and is only there if you are acting under the influence of your inspiration. So when you are feeling the truth on screen or stage you are therefore acting with inspiration. One cannot exist without the other. You will notice that there is a natural progression through using your imagination and belief, The Four Principles, which in turn places you in The State of Being, which releases your inspiration which finally produces truthful emotion.

Truth is so important as it connects you with the audience. When you are truthful the audience will believe everything you do, you will connect with them on an instinctive level. They will feel your truth and will connect with your character, or more specifically with your truth, in the character's circumstances. Without this connection you will be seen as 'acting' or pretending by the audience and this will distance them from your character's life and in turn will drive your audience away from you. There is a very fine balance in the relationship between an actor and the audience. The audience are willing to suspend their disbelief as long as they can feel the truth of the character's life. This is true of Checkov, Ibsen, Brecht, Berkoff, Mamet and Lloyd Webber! The audience are very supportive and are willing to believe even the most extreme circumstances as long as they can feel the truth of the character. This is even evident in Pantomime. The audience know that Jack's Mother is a man dressed as a woman, but they will go along with all the hilarity and outrageous circumstances if they believe that the core of the character's life is truthful. But be aware that real truth can lead to an introspective performance and while this is perfect for the camera it has its limitations on the stage; the actor needs to layer onto that truth further levels of performance which we will discuss later.

CASE STUDY

Whilst I was working on "Little Malcolm and his Struggle against the Eunuchs" as the understudy of two characters in the West End, all the understudies were given the opportunity to do their own performance for friends, families and agents. The characters are written in an almost farcical nature and the character that I was playing, Ingham, was a particularly comical character who had difficulty expressing himself. In this particular scene, the character has been forced by Malcolm, the leader of his own political party, to give false evidence in a pseudo trial of one of their friends. The statement that Ingham has to give includes details of a secret meeting between the friend 'Nipple' and the arch enemy of the party 'Allard'. Ingham obviously hasn't seen any meeting as this was a fabrication but he proceeds to give a faltering statement which consists of cut sentences, actions and insinuations. Whilst I was giving this statement in the performance I felt the confusion, fear and sense of betrayal of Ingham well up from my centre and I was truly in The State of Being and operating under the influence of inspiration. This was an amazing feeling and the emotions that I felt were truthful. As a result, the audience bought into the character's circumstances, believed his pain and found the situation hilarious - which was the intention of the playwright when he wrote this scene.

In life we don't like liars so why should the world of performance be any different? If we encounter a liar in life we don't trust them and instinctively if we don't believe the characters on screen or stage, we won't trust them. This will create a distancing effect between the actor and the audience and they will not suspend their disbelief and connect with the character's circumstances. The audience have a keen sense that can detect liars and the result of this is that they will not buy into the character's life on screen or stage. Ultimately if you do not invest in the truth of the character, you are lying and this then leads the actor to show and not be. This will make the performance false and will drive your audience away from your character's life and circumstances.

The biggest contradiction in our art and craft is that everything is make believe! The job of the actor is to create truth in a non-truthful situation. You have to strive to find truth whilst on stage with an audience watching you, or in front of a camera with the crew watching on an incomplete set. The other problem is that the audience are just as aware of this false situation, whether they are in the auditorium of a theatre or cinema or on their sofa at home watching the TV. They want to be taken away from their surroundings and placed in the world of the performance. This makes the actor's job all the more difficult! Performing is not true so you have to create truth on screen or stage in order to convey the story of the character and over come all these contradictions.

A point to consider is where do the emotions that lead us to truth come from? Have you ever felt an emotion in life so keenly that you can feel it well up from your very centre? Do you feel butterflies in your stomach when you are nervous? Have you been hit by grief so hard that it feels that you have been punched in the stomach? Have you been so full of rage you can feel the anger burst from you like a volcano? What have all these emotions got in common? The answer is that they come from your abdomen. There is some research that suggests that we have another 'brain' that can effect emotions. Apparently humans have another hundred million neurones that line the gut, from the oesophagus to the anus, and it is almost the equivalent size of a cat's brain. It is this 'second brain', known as the enteric nervous system that independently controls the function of the gut. Present in the gut are neurotransmitters including signalling molecules of dopamine, which is associated with pleasure and reward, along with ninety five percent of the body's serotonin which is used to combat depression. It has been discovered that nerve signals from the gut can affect your mood. Although instigated from your brain, the fight or flight response results in blood being diverted from your stomach to other organs in your body and gives you the sensation of 'butterflies'. The litmus test is, when you are performing and feel the emotion rise from inside, you know that you have connected with truthful emotion and what you are feeling is real. Then the audience will believe the life of your character.

Chapter 9
It all comes from you!

"You are enough"

Mark Rylance

It is impossible to create a character from thin air. No matter what you believe, there is no way that you can create truth if you are trying to step into a character's circumstances. It all becomes guess work and is false. Stanislavski suggests that an actor must use the 'If' as a springboard into the imagination, but if you are asking, "what if my character were in this position or circumstance?" you will not be able to find a truthful response. If you ask, "what if I were in this position or circumstance?" again you would have to really stretch your imagination and belief to manage to make that mental leap. Your job is to create truth and the only way to do this is to work from yourself. The emphasis of the 'what if' question is based on make believe and there is not truth in that. You must draw the character to you and ask:

- What is the emotional essence of this moment? What should I be feeling truthfully?
- What Imaginary Circumstance can I imagine and believe in that will give me the truthful emotional response? This is the first of The Four Principles - but more of that later.

These are the most important questions an actor *must* ask themselves. The only way to create truthful emotion is to use yourself.

Without using yourself you will have no real substance to your character. You will be creating a facsimile of the truth. This is the fundamental problem with Stanislavski's assertion of acting, "Truth of the passions, feelings that seem true in the set circumstances"[2]. Truth can only exist if you commit yourself and your own emotions and imagination to a character but if feelings *seem* true then you are not being but you are pretending and therefore you are not being truthful. Another problem is that if you approach the character externally you again distance yourself from the truth. The greatest irony is that Stanislavski was starting to veer towards an external approach as he was drawing to end of his life and Vakhtangov and Myerhold were his proteges in this approach. The assertion is that if you find the absolute essence of an emotion physically it will start to affect you internally if you repeat that physical gesture. The problem with this approach in my opinion is that it really only works in high drama and heightened theatre. It has no place in screen acting which has to come from within. Truth can only come from within the actor. You have to plumb the depths of your psyche and become really honest with yourself. Only you know what you have to imagine in order to elicit a truthful emotional response.

If you don't use yourself then you are merely 'acting'. This is not to say that you have to go down the road of Strasberg's 'Emotion Memory'. It means that your personal fears and joys can be created by yourself if you use the right imaginary stimulus. You can only use yourself and your emotions. You need to practice using different Imaginary Circumstances in order to discover what imaginary triggers you possess that

---

[2] An Actor's Work - Konstantin Stanislavski © Routledge 2008

create truthful emotion. Truthful emotions can only be created from personal investment in the Imaginary Circumstances. It is pointless to identify what triggers you and then not have the gumption to really invest in those ideas because you are scared of what might happen. The rehearsal room is the perfect place to be vulnerable as everyone in the room is after the same thing…an exceptional piece of work. You need to trust your fellow actors and director and allow yourself to be vulnerable. You need to ask yourself how you relate to the emotional journey of the character. You will notice that the script is made up of plot and actions but the key thing to identify is the emotional journey of the character. We will discuss this in more detail when we talk about the text.

Ultimately you need to say the words as opposed to your character saying the words or you saying the character's words. It is an important distinction to make. Only you can react truthfully to your own imagined circumstances. You need to see the character as you but exhibiting different attributes. You need to see your character as you with differing levels of emotion. Maybe you need to have more fear or hate evident to be congruent to your character's actions. You should visualise the differences between yourself and the character in terms of a graphics equaliser (See fig. 3). Each emotion can be made greater or lesser dependent on what the emotional make up of the character is. This is what makes character; the noticeable differences between your own characteristics and the characteristics of the creation of the playwright.

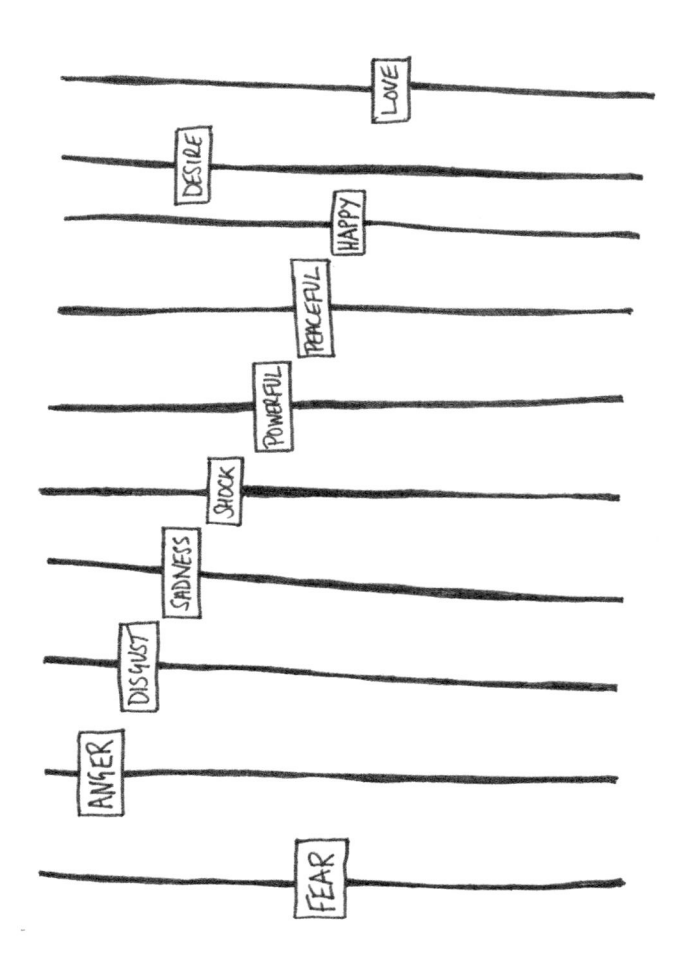

fig.3

THE PROCESS

The key question that you need to ask as an actor is, "How do I make this relate to me?". It is only by drawing the character's world to your imaginary world that you can create a real truthful emotional response. You need to remember that your imagination is boundless. It is only you yourself who can create any limits to it. It is possible to create any human emotion if you use your imagination fully. It is just a matter of really investing in your imagination, challenging yourself and being completely honest with yourself. We have all felt every emotion in our life to one degree or another. Fear, anger, disgust, sadness, shock, powerful, peaceful, happy, desire and love. Granted, probably not to the level that will be required by your character, but you can ramp up the stakes in your Imaginary Circumstances and make it really compelling - you need to create the emotion in its highest form in order for it to affect you. Another attribute that you have at your disposal as an actor is the ability to empathise and sympathise. You can view sympathy as subjective, the ability to feel someone else's emotional state and revel in it, and empathy as a more objective view of understanding why someone is feeling the way they do but not necessarily feeling the emotion yourself. Every human being has these attributes and it is what defines us as humans. The actor has to really employ these to their fullest extent and take advantage of our very human nature.

Only you can discover what Imaginary Circumstances will release a truthful emotional response. It is sometimes helpful to have an acting coach to nudge you in the right direction but their emotional triggers will be different from yours. A truly gifted coach will be able to read you and give you suggestions that are close and then you don't have such a hard time finding the actual trigger to get the desired response. As I have said, you have to be honest with yourself if you are to create truth. If the only way for you to really achieve a truthful emotional state seems depraved or morally wrong, tough! You need to push yourself and be absolutely honest with yourself. It is in your head and not verbalised so no-one needs to know. If for example you are meant to love the character you are playing opposite with your whole body and although they are attractive to you, you are in a serious relationship, it is not cheating if you imagine yourself having graphic sex with them. Neither is it disrespectful to the actor you are working opposite, if you are giving them a truthful emotion then really what you are doing is giving them the respect they deserve. Obviously I am not condoning that you actually try and pursue the scenario that you are creating in your mind, but you need to imagine what will create a truthful response in you unreservedly.

Even if you have not experienced a required emotion in your life, by employing The Four Principles you can create The State of Being and induce your subconscious to release the emotions. If we use the example above where you have to be completely in love with the character opposite you and you are finding it difficult to really capture the truthful emotional state then you need to go through this process and prepare yourself before you perform:

Realisation What is the initial emotional state? If you need to be absolutely, desperately in love it depends on where you are in the relationship. If you are playing Romeo and this is the scene where you must leave Juliet after you have consummated the marriage then you need to be excited (happy), scared (fear), lustful (desire), devastated (sad) and in love. You need to create an imaginary circumstance that

THE PROCESS

would make you feel theses emotions. It doesn't have to be in context with the scene, you need to create something personal to you. You need to consider the previous circumstances and imagine what it was like to make love to Juliet. You can't worry about offending your fellow actor, you need to truthfully imagine what it was like as you had sex and then fell asleep in each others arms. You could also imagine what it would be like making love to someone that you love. You need to imagine what would turn you on and not frame it in the context of what Romeo and Juliet may have done but what you would have done to feel so close that you have given yourself to Juliet and also taken her virginity from her (Romeo has had a few conquests in the past). The point is to not shy from what your imagination will provide.

Personalisation If you cannot find your partner attractive in any way then you need to personalise your partner. Make them someone that you have an infatuation with and would wish to sleep with. Someone who turns you on so you can really see them in place of the partner you are working with.

Visualisation You need to really see Juliet's room. Be aware that if you are discovered you will be killed. What is it that is different from your own environment? Where is the bed, what does it look like now that dawn is breaking. You need to be as specific as you can in order to urge your subconsciousness to free truthful emotions.

Replacement If you have prepared sufficiently you should be in The State of Being but you may find the moment that you actually leave Juliet for the final time with the uncertainty of whether you will ever see her again is hard to really feel. Replace the situation with an imaginary circumstance that you can really believe. Imagine what it would be like to leave a loved one not knowing whether you will ever see them again. It doesn't have to have any relevance to the scene but it must resonate with you.

We will look at The Four Principles in more detail later on. If you follow these simple principles, you will find that you can create truthful emotion, your performance will gain brilliance, you will convince your audience and your fellow actors on screen or stage and you will lift everyone's performance because they will be reacting to a real person.

Chapter 10
We all learn differently

*"If a child can't learn the way we teach,
maybe we should teach the way they learn"*
Ignacio Estrada

Now may be a good time to mention that you all learn differently. The acronym **V.A.R.K**. is what educators will recognise as the term to illustrate this.

VISUAL - Visual stimulus, you see things and learn them, shapes on a page, stage and pictures

AUDITORY - By listening, you learn by listening repeatedly. Being told what to do.

READING - The written word is what you use to learn, whether script or instruction.

KINAESTHETIC - Physical learning. You learn by doing, standing in a certain place when saying something.

Granted, the majority of actors are visual and kinaesthetic but others learn by reading or listening. It is important that you identify how you learn because this can affect how easily you can learn lines and take direction. Also, as you will notice as you follow the steps of The Process, it caters for different learning styles and you may find some aspects easier to implement. If you are not a visual learner and you need to use your imagination, write down your scenarios to ensure that they really permeate your subconscious. You may find that when working with text and you do not learn well with written stimulus you should use colours and search for pictures in the blocks of text to help you break it down. Learning lines by recording them will work better for auditory learners and physically moving around as you learn as opposed to trying to analyse academically will work better for kinaesthetic learners.

CASE STUDY

Whilst directing a piece of Magic Realism, 'Under a Mantle of Stars' by Manuel Puig, one of the actors was having a really hard time understanding the actions of his character. He was playing a robber who had entered a house after pretending that his car had broken down and he and his fiancé needed shelter. The owner of the house invited them in. This robber was wearing a ridiculous false moustache and pretended to be the owner's step daughter's long lost father. This is obviously a rather convoluted and confusing scenario as you can tell by the synopsis. The scene that was giving this actor particular problems was when he removed his moustache the daughter acted as if this was normal and then accepted the robber as a possible lover. Within the bounds of Naturalism or Realism this is too unbelievable, but the premise of Magic Realism is that the audience and characters believe whatever they witness without question. This was really hard for the actor to conceptualise and no matter how I explained it to him, he couldn't grasp the idea. In the end we stopped discussing it and I told him to really invest in the scenario and 'just do it'. As soon as he saw and felt how the scene worked he understood it. All that discussion was a waste of time because he wasn't an auditory learner.

Chapter 11
The power of words

"A powerful agent is the right word"
Mark Twain

Words have an amazing force in life, we are controlled and conditioned by them. They can be used in a positive way or a negative way, nonetheless words have a power over us. If you are told enough that you are worthless or selfish you will start to believe it and act accordingly. We are programmed by words from the moment we are born and depending on how those words are used, these words decide what we believe about ourselves. A parent's words are the most powerful, but words from people that you respect as you grow up also have a very strong effect on you. You can turn the connotations of this into a positive force and affect yourself by using the right words. If we can do this to affect *real* circumstances in life then, with the right powerful words, we can affect the Imaginary Circumstances. If this is the case then it is important as an actor that we choose the right words to describe our character so that we can connect with those emotions. This is the part of the process that allows you to use your intellect as it will in turn affect your heart and allow truthful emotion to occur.

Words affect how we react in any given situation. If we try, then all we are ever going to be able to do is keep trying and not succeed. Likewise if we 'act' then all we are doing is putting something on and pretending or 'acting'. This is why I like the distinction in 'Being'; even the word 'Do' can intimate that you have to actually do something. This can have a negative impact on your performance as you are striving to do something and are not **LEAVING** yourself alone, allowing your truthful emotions and instinct do the work. To discover the power of words, all you need to do is remember back to an argument where someone has called you pathetic or fat. Those words can have a profound effect on you, especially if those are words that you constantly heard from people whom you respected!

Words contain the power of emotions. Obvious examples of this are love and hate but words have the power to affect you or someone else, so choose them well. They are so useful to an actor. You will see later when we discuss the Pathway that the right word in the right place can create clarity and make your job as an actor easier. Stella Adler focused on actions when teaching her actors and you can use transitive verbs to clarify your journey through a text, but it all boils down to words; the right words can give you that initial spark that will lead to understanding. The only problem with this approach is that your script and mind can become cluttered with too many words. You need to make things as straightforward as you can when working with text so when we come to breaking it down you need to remember that the right words will really help and always be succinct. The best words to use are emotive words. There is a tendency to be too cerebral when you are selecting words to help your journey through the text and this in the end can become an obstacle. You should use words that describe an emotion: anger, fear, joy as opposed to words that are too complex. Emotions can all be distilled into ten key or primary states, all other emotions find their root in these. We will discuss the ten base emotions later in the book.

THE PROCESS

Other exercises that you can use to create the internal life of the character are the Seven Questions and Internal Rhythm. These exercises are a very reliable way to create the depth to your characterisation and we will explore them in subsequent chapters.

Chapter 12
The power of the mind

"Whatever the mind of a man can conceive and believe, it can achieve."

Napoleon Hill

Part of The Process that has a huge impact on an actor not only on stage but in auditions and to an extent on their career is understanding the power of the mind. When training foundation students for auditions at Drama School part of The Process is to get them to really be open to this concept. In our cynical society it is easy to have a negative attitude to life. It is so important that we are in the right frame of mind all the time in order to progress. If you go into an audition or the first day of rehearsal thinking that you do not deserve to be there then there is no doubt that you will have a bad experience. I'm not saying that you have to have to be arrogant and over confident but you need to have the right mental attitude. If you walk into an audition, confident, happy and positive knowing that the role is right for you and believing that you already have the job, nine times out of ten you will get the job. I have experienced it and it really works!

What you think can really affect your life. If you believe what people say enough, it actually happens. The worst voice to listen to is yourself! This Inner Critic is a voice that can paralyse the actor, it can make you question yourself and then destroy your performance. This is a very hard concept to give credence to but you will find that if you have the right mental state in work and in auditions you will feel the impact.

THE PROCESS

CASE STUDY

Whilst covering in 'Little Malcolm & His Struggle Against The Eunuchs' I managed to get myself into a really negative mindset and this impacted on my work and life. I had decided foolishly that the job was unworthy of me and not only did I miss out on opportunities within the job, I found my auditions were going badly. I managed to wind myself up so much that I missed out on performing with the cast twice. One thing after another seemed to go wrong and all this from believing in the wrong thing and allowing the negative mindset take over. Conversely, after I had finished working in the West End for a year I felt very confident and felt that I had finally proved myself in the industry. The result of this was that with every audition that I had thereafter I was offered the job. I was on a roll and I couldn't be stopped!

It is essential that whether you are an experienced actor or new to the business, the right mindset is absolutely imperative. It can make or break your career so really ensure that you invest the time before you audition or work to believe in yourself and your ability. If you say to yourself, "I'll never get that job, it's too big for me" then I guarantee that you will not get the job! It is a self fulfilling prophesy. If you say you can't, then you can't. You have already given in so there is no way you will succeed. Once you are in the right mental space you will attract what you want.

So how do you manage to get in the right mindset and make all of these wonderful things happen? The key to this is Visualisation, if you commit to ideas then they will succeed.

One thing that I have found that works really well with students when they are auditioning and not managing to get recalls or offers is to get them to create a self-belief poster. I get the student to get a big piece of paper, and write on it phrases like, "I am Brilliant, I am the best at what I do", "I am looking forward to my place at Drama School". Then I get them to put images of what they want on the sheet until it is a colourful collection of phrases and desires but in the present tense, not "I want" or "will have", but "I have". Once they have created this, I get them to stick it in a place where they see it last thing at night and first thing in the morning. If they do this and really believe what they have created, invariably the next audition that they have results in a recall or offer. As weird and wonderful as this sounds, it works. The key thing is to believe. Try it and you will see there is a difference in your life.

Another method that can help you get into the right mindset is to create a mood board with visual images of what you wish to have or be. Place it somewhere you will see it everyday and take time in your day to look at it and experience what those images mean to you. It takes time but if you trust in it you will find that you will get out of a negative mindset and become much more positive and in turn things will change in your life.

The final exercise that you can try is a visual pyramid. Before you go to sleep at night, clear your mind of the daily grind and imagine where you want to end up in your life, what does it look like when you are as successful as you wish to be. For example you may want to be the most successful actor you can be (well you have taken the first step by reading this book!), picture yourself accepting your Oscar, your BAFTA or your Olivier. See it in detail, *be specific*! Next imagine what the step was before you became that successful, then imagine what was the step before that and so on. Eventually you will have created a Pathway to your success. If you imagine that the first steps are at the bottom of a pyramid and that your final position is at the top of the pyramid, you will have a clear journey. Once you have created this image every night re-visualise the pyramid and imagine yourself moving up to your final success.

Over time all of these methods will alter your mindset and you will find that you will gain more success and feel more confident in your ability as a performer and pretty soon there will be no stopping you!

# PART 2

THE PROCESS

HEAD

SECTIONING
NEEDS
PATHWAY — 10 EMOTIONS
7 Q?s
3 RQ?s
RESEARCH
MODEL
WHY ME?

Chapter 13
The Head

"The mind is everything. What you think you become."
                                                    Buddha

As I previously stated, The Process has three separate sections which, when followed, help to create a truthful and believable character. The first of the three main sections of The Process focuses on The Head. This part of the approach includes all the analytical work that you do as an actor. There is no time to analyse during performance as you shouldn't be using your head when you are performing, as I will explain later.

Approaching a Text
When an actor starts a job the first thing they receive is the script. This is a treasure trove of clues and hints and it is the source of the character. This is where the character first comes from.The writer painstakingly creates a world and inhabits it with people and it is their unravelling story that is the basis of the film or play. Scripts are character driven stories and the actor's job is to bring these words to life as a three dimensional human being. Therefore the text is the most important starting point. If the actors are creating a new piece then the characters come first and a story will develop from their experiences. Mike Leigh creates work in this way and the level of truth his characters have occurs because he works with his actors first creating real characters and then he weaves a story from their lives.

There are some very simple tools available to the actor in order for them to draw the most from the script and really understand the character they are creating. The first thing to do is to read the play or script, then read it again and then again. Really make sure you are familiar with the complete story and you will start to see how all pieces of your character's life fit together. There are some who think that you should not really know what is going to happen to your character as this reflects real life. I contend that you are going to know what happens to your character before you perform anyway and if you are working in film you will be shooting out of sequence so the better you know the script the easier you will find it. You need to dissect the text for clues and become a detective. There are clues that are sprinkled throughout the text and all of these are like gold dust as they will really help you develop the life of your character. You will find out other characters' opinions of your character, you will find the inner most secrets of your character, you will discover their attitude to others and their own circumstances. If you are working with Shakespeare, look at the language used. Shakespeare's scripts tell an actor everything, not only what they are thinking but also what they are doing. There are many books on how to approach Shakespeare and Cicely Berry has many exercises that you should look up.

Whilst you are reading you need to be aware of the period of the piece as this will have an effect on how you perform your character. In the Eighteenth century people moved very differently from how we do now, so you need to couple your text work with research. You need to remember that there is a very close relationship between an actor and the text. They share a symbiotic relationship which leads to art. The key thing to discern is the emotional content of the script. Do not over analyse. This is not an English Literature task, it is performance, so you need to really understand the emotional journey of your character and the other characters that affect you.

Stanislavski says that the text gives the actor the 'Given Circumstances.' The 'Given Circumstances' are what you are given by the writer. The circumstances of the world of the script. It is everything that is contained in the words, the details of the world of the script and the the characters in that world. The 'Given Circumstances' are all that the actor is given and this is the starting point when you create the character. It is the blueprint of the script and the world that you and the director are going to create. This is applicable to any script you are working with from Shakespeare to Musical Theatre.

Once you have read the script a number of times make it personal to you. You have to bridge the gap between the writer's ideas and the truth that you will create in performance. The closer you bring the text to you the easier it is to create the life of the character. You will be using your imagination to create Imaginary Circumstances that echo the 'Given Circumstances' of the script. Don't use memories because, as we have discussed, these are not a reliable source from which to draw a truthful emotion. Use people from your life and create Imaginary Circumstances that draw an emotional reaction from you.

Sectioning
So what do you need to do once you have read your script? It is important that you break down the whole script into Sections to make it easier to digest. This is based on Stanislavski's 'Bits' but has been simplified to ensure that the actor's work through the script is uncluttered. Usually you will have a script already broken down into scenes. What you need

THE PROCESS

to do is to split each scene into smaller Sections. These are usually determined by entrances and exits of characters and by changes in the thoughts of your character. The focus of the Sections has to be from your character's point of view as they are there to help you find your way through the script and story of the character. In some Sections you will have monologues, it is important that you Section these too. When there is a major change of thought or tack by your character create a new Section (see fig. 4).

fig.4

Needs

In life we have needs. As you are reading this book perhaps your need is to find a way to become a truthful actor. Everyday is filled with our needs, I need to get a better job, I need to impress this person, I need to eat and so on. Therefore a character has to have Needs in their life. Stanislavski refers to this as an 'Objective' or a want, but as you have already discovered, words play an important part in how we perceive life. I feel that a want or objective isn't a strong enough motivation for an actor. If you need something it becomes important to your existence so you will work your hardest to achieve it. Initially it is important to define what the character's overall Need is for the play and write it down. This is always termed in the first person 'I need…' to ensure that you are as close to your character as possible and you do not create a barrier by looking from the outside in. If we use The Crucible as an example, once you have read the play you should realise that an overall Need for John Proctor could be, 'I need to keep my good name'. This is regardless of the fact that he has sullied his name by having an affair with Abigail Williams because this is his overall Need and he will strive for this throughout the play. Abigail Williams' overall Need might be, 'I need to escape punishment'. Now your character's Needs will change throughout the script but you need to identify the overall Need that drives the character's actions. Why do they do the things that they do? Once the overall Need is identified, you must find a Need for each scene. It's important to note that these Needs should be congruous with the character's overall Need. It doesn't make sense if John Proctor's Need in one scene is to seduce Abigail Williams again because his overall Need is to protect his reputation and name. We may make choices in life that seem to contradict our overall Need, but if you look closer at those actions you can see that they are still tied in with that overall Need. Therefore as in life, so in art; our job is to create truth on screen or stage so what we would do in life we need to replicate when we are 'acting' or as I prefer to say: Being (See fig. 5).

fig.5

Pathway

After you have Sectioned your scenes and identified your character's Needs for each scene, you need to create the Pathway for your character's journey. In order to do this we need to look at the Ten Emotions. As I mentioned earlier, every emotion can be traced back to ten base emotions: fear, anger, disgust, sadness, shock, powerful, peaceful, happy, desire and love. These are the purest and most simple form of the emotions. Complex emotions such as jealousy can find their root in either anger or fear and there is a danger of being too cerebral when choosing an emotion for each section - remember to Keep It Simple, Stupid! A useful tool to use to help you start to identify what base emotion you require is the emotion wheel. This is by no means an exhaustive list but it is a good place to start (see fig. 6)

THE PROCESS

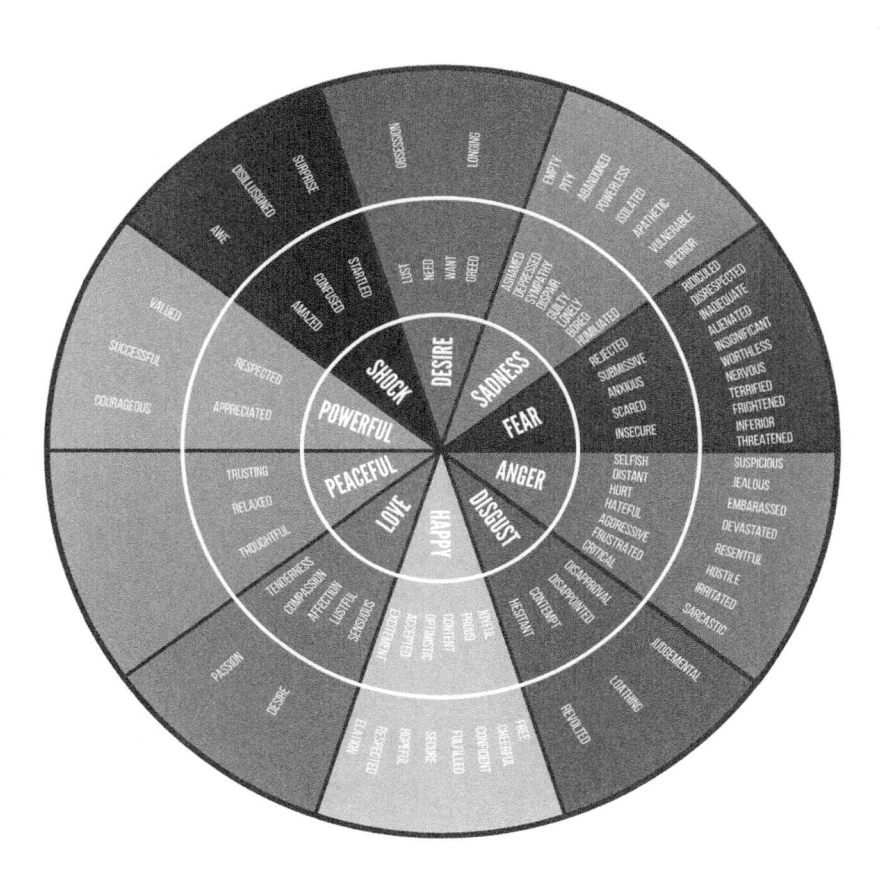

fig.6

The next thing that you need to do is to identify what is the emotion the moment before you open your mouth in the scene. By deciding what emotion your character feels before they speak you are working towards The State of Being. After you have attributed an emotion to the moment before you speak, you put an asterisk on your script and then write the word. Once you have done this you need to decide which of the Ten Emotions is appropriate for each of the Sections and write the emotion on your script (see fig. 7 showing final Sectioned script).

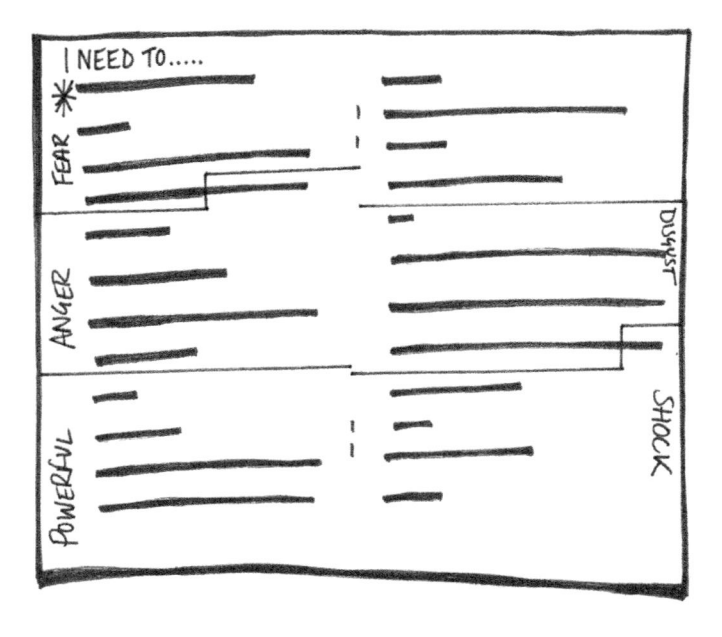

fig. 7

THE PROCESS

When you have completed annotating your script you will see that you have a very simple Pathway for your character. The effect of this is that you are not faced with blocks of text but can see a simple journey through the script. It is worth remembering that these emotions could change, because when you perform you may discover that your initial choices may not work. You are a living human being and your character needs to reflect that too. With that in mind you can approach this element, and only this element of The Process, in a more generalised way. The emotions of the character are fluid so you need to be able to change them as you react to the other characters in the scene.

This is just a starting point so don't get too attached to these emotional keywords. However they are important in order to make you think more practically and to stop you thinking analytically. You can use these emotional keywords as a basis for your Realisation when you are creating the truthful journey of your character. It is vital that you use pencil as throughout the rehearsal process things change. If you write down these emotions in pen, subconsciously you are saying that the choices are immutable and therefore you will find that you may have a block and be unable to adapt the emotion in response to your partner or partners in the scene. It is no good if you decide how you are going to play your character without taking into account how the other characters in the scene will interact with you and affect you. Performing is a living medium so you need to be able to adapt. Things change, one day your instinct may lead you in a slightly different direction and this in turn will have an impact on your fellow actors. In life, even if you repeat the same things every day, there are subtle differences to your routine or how you feel towards a fellow co-worker so you need to be prepared for this to happen in performance.

Once you have broken down your script you are ready to use it to help you create the basis of your character. Following are a series of exercises that help you flesh out the character from the text and give you an outline on which to base the next element of The Process.

The Seven Questions

These questions are used to give an immediate response to the 'Given Circumstances'. It is important to be as specific as you can in your response. One word answers will not help you much! Be inventive, but use the context of the piece. You need to be imaginative but you are defining the truth of the character as given to you by the playwright. These questions are asked in the first person in order to bring your character closer to you. Write the responses down in a workbook that you can refer to if needs be.

Who am I?
Think of the detail. Age, education, experiences that affect you, social status. Don't forget simple things like full name, family situation and so on. The more you give yourself the more you can respond to.

Where am I?
As Stella Adler comments in her book 'The Art of Acting', Stanislavski thought that the where was vital to evoking a truthful response when creating character. Visualisation is an extension of this principal. Again, be detailed, think about what the environment looks like as well as naming where you

are. Don't just say 'On a street corner'. Which city, which town, which village? What does this environment mean to you? Is it home? Is it a strange place? How do you feel about it? If it is a room, whose room? How do you feel about being here? Blanche Dubois is going to feel different to her sister Stella when standing in the Kowalski's front room.

When is it?
What time of day? What year? What season? Have there been any significant events that have had an effect on you? Is anything related to the time of the world in which you, as your character, exist?

What do I need?
This is the driving force for your character as previously discussed.

Why do I need it?
This is the justification for your Need. You will find this in the text. We all need something for some reason whether it be altruistic or selfish.

How am I going to get it?
The character's actions will justify how you achieve your need, but you may need to imagine how you will get it if your character fails in the text.

What must I overcome?
We all have obstacles that can prevent us from getting what we want and this is the same for our characters. Use the text initially to find out what this may be. If you have no obstacle then you will invariably achieve your Need.

These questions are intended to form a tangible world for you in the world of the text. The more detailed you are the clearer the picture you will get. The key thing to remember is that this work is intended as a starting point. Once you have answered these questions you will be able to develop your ideas and your imagination will create circumstances that you will respond to with truthful emotion. As with all of the more academic or cerebral elements of The Process they are intended as a rehearsal tool and once they have been worked on should be allowed to inform you on a subconscious level and therefore not be dwelt upon when performing.

Relationships: the Three Questions

Relationships are the single most important element of our lives as a human being. They shape who we are, what we think about ourselves, what others think about us and how we operate with different people. It is essential therefore that you spend time trying to unlock all the relationships that your character has and find a way to replicate them in performance. Relationships define us in life so we must have them on screen or stage and nurture them in rehearsal. It is important to note that how our character interacts with others on screen or stage defines how we are perceived by our audience. If we are truly meant to love the other character we are playing opposite, it is essential that we take some time to discover what that looks and feels like. Imagine how bad it would be if there was no believable relationship between Romeo and Juliet! It is your job to define the relationship and then develop it between the characters. It is important to note that a truthful relationship on screen or stage helps to deepen your own characterisation as you will start to completely believe in the world that you have created. This will then allow you to convince your sub-conscious that what you are doing is real and therefore allow you to find the inspiration to create truthful emotions. Relationships have a place in both the Head and the Heart of The Process. Initially you need to use the script to gain a clear understanding of how you feel towards the other characters in the world of the play or film. Once you have completed this you can explore the reality of the relationships as you continue to develop your character's inner life.

So, how do we actually discover the relationships of the characters in the text? Initially you have to become a detective and tease out all the information provided to you by the playwright. You need to read the text and answer these key questions:

What do other characters say about my relationships?
Include the key characters that you have close relationships to, such as partners, spouses and so on.

What do I say about my relationships?
Scour the text to find any comments you make about other key characters and decide what that means about how you treat them.

What do my relationships say about me?
Once you have discovered everything you can from the text, analyse what you say about other characters to define how you react to them.

All of this information can be gathered and will help you create a picture of how your character reacts to other characters in the world of the play.

Research
Once you have scoured the text and gleaned as much information as you can it is important that you actually engage in research for your character. Things that you should consider include:

Job
I wouldn't expect you to go and work as a cab driver in New York like Robert De Niro in the film "Taxi Driver", but it is important that you have a working understanding of what you character does as a job if you are going to create a truthful world in which your character exists. There are times when this is not possible because your character may be non-naturalistic, but if you are meant to be a doctor in an Emergency Room, watch documentaries and get yourself familiar with their way of life, language and so on.

Hobbies or pastimes
If your character is meant to have a passion of which you have no experience, then do as much research as you can to get yourself acquainted with it. For example, if they are an avid collector of anything, research what that is, try to understand why they collect what they do.

Skills
If your character has particular skills that you do not, discover how they develop them or become proficient in them, whether it is playing a musical instrument or carpentry.

Time Period
It is essential that you understand the time period in which your character lives and operates. This is not such an issue if your piece is set in the present day, but if it is an historical

piece it is essential that you understand the social conventions of that period and how your character operates within them.

Environment

Look into where your character lives and works. Try and discover what it is like to live in such an environment, particularly if it is different from your own. What are the factors that make an impression on your character's life? Are they happy where they live and work? Do they feel safe or threatened?

Obviously you won't always have time in a contract to go into too much great detail, but it is your job to provide a truthful character that operates in a real world and as such you need to be able to understand their world as completely as you can. This work should be done whether you are working in film or stage, it will help you to fully understand your character and present a truthful life in front of camera or on stage.

Model

Having a visual cue for your character can really inspire you as it gives you something concrete to focus on. Find a picture of someone who you think your character looks like, it could be an actor, a picture of someone from the newspaper or internet, just pin it down and be specific. Once you have found the right image put it into a workbook and refer to it before you start to rehearse or perform. This is a very powerful tool as it communicates with your subconscious and can really help to coax your inspiration during performance.

Why me?

The last thing that you should do when working on the script is identify what your actual purpose is in the world of the script. The playwright puts characters in for a reason so you need to identify what that purpose is. Armed with that information you can check that your Needs are correct and you can identify your purpose. This is one of the greatest gifts that you get from creating a character in a play or script. If you could know your own purpose in life imagine what choices you would make! Take advantage of this, as once you identify what your character's purpose is you will understand their actions. Remember hindsight is 20:20 so armed with this knowledge you will be able to develop a complete picture of your character's motivations and needs.

THE PROCESS

HEART

THE 4 PRINCIPLES
IMAGINARY PAST
RELATIONSHIPS
INTERNAL RAYTHM

Chapter 14 - The Heart

"Never go on empty"
Sanford Meisner

Once you have analysed and broken down your script, you are ready to move to the central and most important part of The Process, the Heart. This is where the truth is created and the inner life of your character is made. Whilst it is imperative that you stop using the Mind element of The Process in performance, you must always use the Heart.

The Four Principles

At the centre of The Process are The Four Principles. This is the secret of acting and when fully applied transforms the actor's performance from good to amazing! When used properly, actors and acting students, have been able to captivate an audience and produce truthful emotions that affect both themselves and the spectators. These principles are the most import elements for creating character and must be used if an actor wishes consistently to create truthful emotions and therefore truthful performances. The Four Principles use the actor's imagination to the full and if used properly and committed to fully, are guaranteed to ensure the actor is in The State of Being and as so is performing under the influence of Inspiration. The principles are: Realisation, Personalisation, Visualisation, and Replacement (See fig. 8.).

THE PROCESS

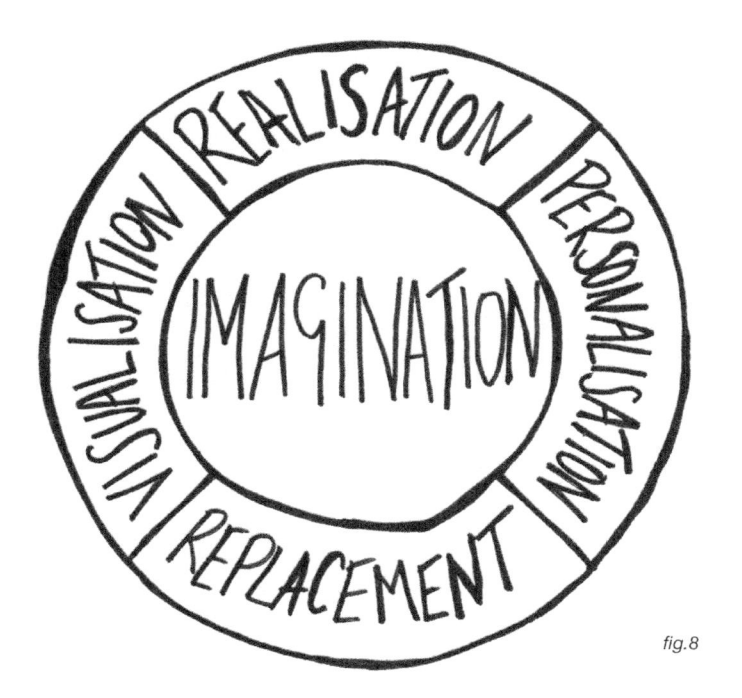

fig.8

Realisation

In this chapter we will discuss the first of the principles: Realisation. This is the first opportunity an actor gets to really use his or her imagination during performance and it is the best way to get into The State of Being. It is used in order to prepare the actor fully before they start to perform. Whether working with text or improvisation it is imperative that you prepare. As you know, once in The State of Being you will be able to respond truthfully to emotions in the scene or speech. You will react truthfully and really feel your emotions.
Realisation is the spark of inspiration, which will then develop into full inspiration once you fully get into the state.
Realisation is similar to Stanislavski's 'If' but instead of the

springboard into the imagination, it is the springboard into the truth and the emotional world of the character.

Realisation sets the tone of your performance, it is something that you must do before you enter or say your first line. You are imagining a situation prior to the moment you appear on screen or stage. Instead of trying to imagine what actually happened as the character, you are recreating the first emotional state you identified when creating the Pathway prior to speaking or entering a scene. This will put you into The State of Being. To do this you need to use your imagination. As explained earlier, it is impossible to completely transform into a character. You need to draw the character to you in order to create truthful emotions. Initially you need to decide what emotion the character is feeling before opening his or her mouth. Once you have identified this you need to engage your imagination and create an Imaginary Circumstance that would induce the required emotion in you. You need to imagine something personal to you. You are not using 'Emotion Memory' for the reasons discussed earlier. Remember that you are going to create something really compelling that will give you some real truth. It has to be something that will really affect you and make you react with truthful emotion. You need to replay this imaginary circumstance in your mind's eye again and again until you feel the truth of the emotion.

Example

Say that your character is about to confront their lover with the discovery of an affair. Ask yourself what would be the emotional state of your character before they enter? Let's say betrayed. If you trace this to one of the Ten Base Emotions it would be anger. In your Realisation you need to create an

THE PROCESS

imaginary circumstance where you would feel this emotion. Use your lovers or friends. You would need to really up the stakes so make the person that your lover is having an affair with is your sibling or your best friend. Imagine the events that have taken place. Be specific. Imagine everything to the most intimate detail. Then imagine that the rest of your family knew and were hiding it from you. How do you feel now? Once you have connected fully with the emotion, then you are ready to start the scene or enter. This will put you into The State of Being and you will then be able to react to your fellow performer with truth. As you start to imagine the scenario you will gradually start to feel the emotion well up inside you. It is important not to start your performance too soon or too late. You need to gauge when the emotion is at its zenith, the highest point it can be at. Once you have reached the zenith you need to ride the wave of the emotion. Commit to it fully, don't hold back. It is important that you try this in rehearsal first or in an environment where you feel safe. I have seen students who start to feel the emotion and keep pushing it until it starts to become false. It is a delicate process and requires a lot of practice until you can feel just the right moment to launch into your performance.

CASE STUDY

In a one to one session I was working with a young student on his monologue for Drama School. This young man had brought in a piece that was typically larger than life with loads of emotion and a great deal of shouting. Needless to say this was not really an appropriate speech selection. I gave him a fresh piece about a young boy who had been abandoned by his father at the zoo. Initially on the surface this speech had nothing really in common with the student and so he was finding it difficult to connect with the material. After a bit of digging around I encouraged him to identify the first emotion of the speech and then create an Imaginary Circumstance that would get him into The State of Being. After some time he discovered something that worked for him (it is important to say that Realisation is very personal and it is only through a lot of personal soul searching and honesty with yourself that the right initial stimulus can be found) and then he immediately found a way into the emotional state of the character. This put him in the perfect state to be able to respond further with the rest of the speech, the result of which was that he ended up performing with such honesty that we both ended up in tears as if the events that had transpired in the speech had actually happened to us! It is important to note that if the actor is feeling the emotion truthfully, the audience will be drawn to them and feel the emotion as they empathise with the character on stage.

EXERCISE

Emotional Realisation Sit in a chair or lie down with the soles of your feet on the ground and your knees pointing up to the ceiling. Close your eyes and let your mind go blank. Decide on one of the Ten Emotions and start to imagine a scenario that would make you feel that emotion. Make it compelling and as extreme a scenario as you can. Do not try and use a memory - create the scenario from your imagination. Keep playing the scenario over and over again like a movie in your mind's eye. It is essential that you are honest with yourself, don't shy away from images that really affect you. Once you feel the emotion, choose another of the Ten Emotions and repeat the process. You will find that once you have felt one emotion creating the next one becomes a little bit easier.

Repeat this exercise until you can feel all ten of the emotions. You should repeat this exercise regularly so that you can discover the triggers that spark off each emotion.

If you find that a trigger or imaginary scenario stops being effective just try something new. That's the beauty of the imagination.

Personalisation

The second of The Four Principles is a very powerful tool for helping an actor to believe and remain in The State of Being. If you have used Realisation effectively you are well on the way to producing truthful reactions but you will find that you will come across other characters on screen or stage that you will be unable to react to truthfully. Personalisation helps you to believe in your situation. Without a real connection it is impossible to get a truthful emotion when you work with other actors on screen or stage. You can't just pretend you have to have a connection. You must create a connection you can believe in by personalising the situation. It is only then that you will react truthfully with real emotion. Personalising a situation forces a truthful reaction. If, for example, you are playing a part where you need to feel the loss of a loved one, then you must imagine that the person you have lost is someone from your life, a loved one or family member for instance. It is only if you truly believe this to be the case that you will coax your sub-conscious to release the real emotions and you will feel them as if it were true.

CASE STUDY

The student who was working on the speech where he was abandoned by his father was really having difficulty connecting with his speech when it came to describing the moment his father left him. In his own life his father and mother had split but this is something he had dealt with over the years. This meant he couldn't use his personal experience, he had to imagine something. I told him to distance himself from the image and replace the young character with someone else, his brother perhaps. This was what he needed to then be affected emotionally. In his mind he saw his father leave his young brother, for whom he had subsequently felt responsible, and the desolation of a young child losing his father came to him with full force and so he responded with real emotion.

If you are being generalised with your approach to other characters on screen or stage then your acting will be generalised. You cannot have a faceless person in your mind if you are talking about a loved one or indeed talking to someone who is meant to be a loved one. Be specific. Use people from your life. If you need to be madly in love with someone and you don't have any of those feelings for the actor you are playing opposite, then imagine it is someone you are infatuated with. It can be someone you met or even a famous person that you secretly lust after. No one will know what is in your head so use it to full advantage and be honest with yourself. Create a face for each character you play against or mention on screen or stage. You will respond with emotional truth if you really believe you are looking at a loved one or friend. You need to literally superimpose their face over the face of the person you are working opposite or thinking about.

EXERCISE

Firstly read out loud the following poem without thinking. Feel the rhythm and the tempo and just let the words do their work.

Stop all the clocks, cut off the telephone,
Prevent the dog from barking with a juicy bone,
Bring out the coffin, let the mourners come.

Let aeroplanes circle moaning overhead
Scribbling on the sky the message, "He is Dead".
Put crepe bows round the white necks of the public doves,
Let the traffic policemen wear black cotton gloves.

He was my North, my South, my East and West,
My working week and my Sunday rest,
My noon, my midnight, my talk, my song;
I thought that love would last forever: I was wrong.

The stars are not wanted now; put out every one,
Pack up the moon and dismantle the sun,
Pour away the ocean and sweep up the wood;
For nothing now can ever come to any good.[3]

Now imagine that you are talking about someone close to you. Really see them and ensure that it is someone from your own life, be specific, really see them and imagine they are opposite you. Imagine every detail that you can about them, their face, eyes, hair, physicality and so on.

---

[3] Funeral Blues is Copyright © 1936 by W.H. Auden.

Now as you see them in your mind's eye, read the poem out loud again and notice how your emotions will start to engage. Finally imagine the person you may have lost that the poem is talking about. It doesn't have to be someone you have lost but possibly someone you would hate to lose. Again imagine them in every detail. Do not resort to actual memories but do imagine people from your life (remember my example about my daughter and guilt), be brave and honest.

Now read out the poem to your imaginary person about the imaginary person you lost.

You should notice how the real emotion will rise and you will feel the real sense of loss.

CASE STUDY

When I was in my final year of Drama School one of my final performances was as Abraham in Tony Harrison's 'The Mysteries'. For those of you unfamiliar with this bible story, Abraham is asked by God to offer his son Isaac as a sacrifice to him. Abraham obviously wants to prove his faith to God so takes his son up a mountain to sacrifice him. He is about to do it when God stops him and is pleased with his faith. Now this is all well and good but the actor who was playing my son was someone who I didn't care for at all and he didn't care for me either, in fact we really hated each other at that point. So I had to try and find a way to convey my total love for the child and my complete desperation at the fact that I had to kill him when in reality I couldn't feel any favourable emotion for this actor at all. Now, to be honest, this actor was working really well playing in a childish and naive way with his toy dinosaur so he was giving me something to work with. The only way I could conjure up a truthful emotion and not 'act' at loving this actor was to superimpose the face of my youngest brother on

THE PROCESS

his and use my imagination fully so that I could trick my subconscious into to releasing truthful emotions. As a result I created a very poignant scene which really affected the audience, and I gained a first for that particular performance.

The importance of Personalisation cannot be overlooked as it is a really powerful way of creating emotion and keeping you in The State of Being.

Both Personalisation and Visualisation can be used to support your Realisation. If you imagine someone particular in your life that you are about to interact with and specifically imagine where you are before you start to perform, you can add to the Imaginary Circumstances you have created and unlock your inspiration (See fig. 9).

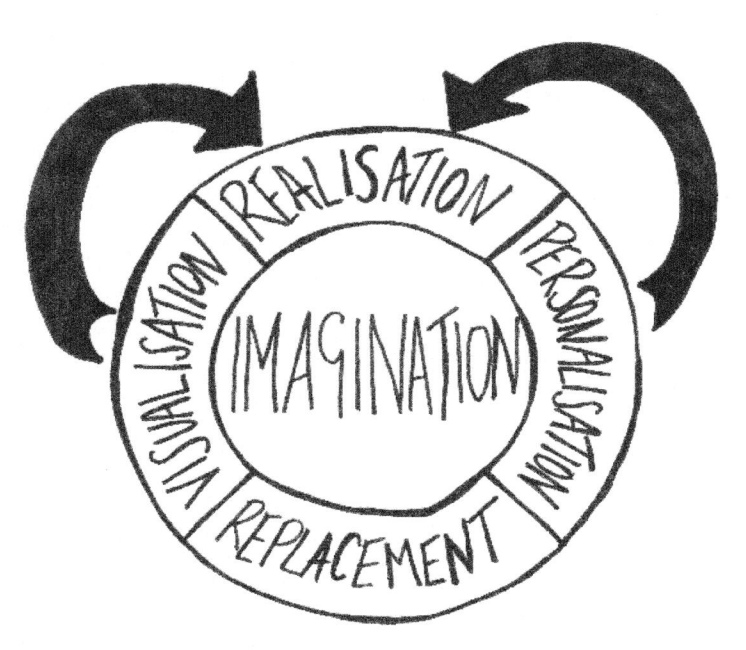

fig.9

Visualisation

This is the third of The Four Principles and it really supports Realisation. So, suppose you have decided what your first emotional state is and have started to feel the truth of that emotion. You are at a very delicate part of getting into The State of Being, anything can break your creative flow and once that happens everything can come crashing down like a house of cards. Don't worry because if you use Visualisation effectively you can bolster your Realisation and ensure that is is a solid foundation to work from.

In Stella Adler's book 'The Art of Acting', Stella goes to great pains to describe her time in Paris working with Stanislavski and how he was adamant that the key thing that an actor should be aware of was the 'Where'. Where the character is during each scene and the complete world of the character on the stage. Similarly, visualising the character's environment during your Realisation is a particularly effective way of keeping you in The State of Being. This is an essential step in creating the truth; if you fully create the world in your imagination you will react to your situation truthfully. The 'Where' is essential if you want to create the correct emotion. The 'Where' is an essential aspect of creating a world you can believe in that tricks your subconscious so you create emotions truthfully. You need to create and totally visualise the world around you. Depending on the situation you can either imagine the world of the character or a place that you could imagine having the same type of conversation. Whichever gives you the strongest emotional response. Be specific and paint as vivid a picture as you can. You really need to see that world in all its glory. This is helped by set when you are on stage, but if you are delivering a speech to camera, in an audition or in a piece that has very little set, it is something that will support your creative endeavours and help you remain in The State of Being.

The other great use of Visualisation is that it can really help if you feel that you are losing the emotional connection with your role. If this happens, invariably it is because you are focussing on yourself, seeing where you are doing things wrong, criticising you performance and so on. This is deathly as it really pulls you out of The State of Being and starts to make you introspective. When performing you have to perform to someone or something so you don't become introverted. By visualising fully you are directing your attention away from you, you are 'giving' which means that your audience or your screen or stage partner will react and give you something back to react to. This is what happens in life, we affect others and their reactions affect us so we must do the same when we are performing.

EXERCISE

Sit in a quiet space and clear your mind. Decide on a room or place that you know really well and with which you are very familiar. In your mind start to recreate the place. Be specific. Paint every detail in your imagination. Picture colours, items, furnishings and so on. Once you have re-created this space and you can believe that you are actually in that space you can bring yourself back into the room.
Repeat this exercise regularly so that when you need to you can recall these spaces quickly. When you perform you can recall these rooms or places to fool your subconscious that you are in a familiar place and it will release truthful emotions.

CASE STUDY

One female student I was working with on a speech was having difficulty with the text because she was describing an event where she sees her boyfriend's mother set alight with a fire bomb in her bedroom whilst she stands helplessly outside the house. She had used her realisation correctly but found that she could not stay in The State of Being when she came to this particular passage. This is where I told her to be brave and really use her imagination and visualise the scene in great detail. I told her to visualise where she was standing, what the house looked like, what the furniture in the bedroom was like, its colours, whether it was outdated or new and so on. Then I asked her to visualise this woman starting to be engulfed in flames and to imagine what it really looked like. This was a particularly harrowing scene that she needed to imagine but she committed to it and she found that she had the apposite emotional reaction and her performance became incredibly real.

Replacement

The final principal is Replacement. This element is particularly useful if you find that you have difficulty with a particular aspect of the script. If you don't get the character's behaviour, reaction or the situation that they are in you can use Replacement to help you. Sometimes the text needs you to create a certain emotion but you cannot create it. If you create a different Imaginary Circumstance that creates the right emotional response, you will be able to produce what the text demands of you. The great thing about this element is that, like Realisation, you don't have to stick to the context of the play. You can create an Imaginary Circumstance that works for you.

THE PROCESS

CASE STUDY
One of my adult acting students was performing Jill's monologue from Lee Hall's 'Cooking with Elvis' where she describes the circumstances around her attempted suicide. The student was having difficulty connecting with the concept of the helplessness she felt as the character as she wakes up in a hospital bed next to her mother after the suicide attempt. What I asked her to do was to create an imaginary scenario that would make her feel completely helpless rather than trying to relate to the scenario in the text. This immediately changed her approach as instead of trying to wrestle with a scenario that she could find nothing in common with, she took control and created something that elicited a truthful emotional response.

Replacement keeps your performance alive and allows you to use your own emotions to access truth. It also keeps you in The State of Being. As you are aware, truth appears when you have a genuine emotion and by replacing a personalised scenario with the circumstances of the text you can elicit a truthful response from yourself.

So what is Replacement? It is like Realisation in as much as it is using your imagination to create an Imaginary Circumstance that you can work with that will elicit the appropriate emotion from you for a section of the text that you cannot just react to instinctively. If, for example, you are Hamlet and you are performing the scene when Hamlet is confronting his mother Gertrude for marrying his uncle too soon after her husband's death but you cannot feel the disgust for your mother, all you need to do is to create an Imaginary Circumstance where you would feel absolutely disgusted and disappointed and hurt at your mother or a matriarchal figure in your life (who you have personalised). Again it is something that is incredibly personal but in your heart of hearts you know what would make you feel that way towards your own mother.

Never adhere slavishly to the context of the text, use all the faculties of your imagination in order to coax a truthful emotive response from yourself. The great thing is that a scene can be a collection of Replacements which you can use to propel you through the piece. Again as with Realisation, you can bolster your Replacement by using Personalisation and Visualisation (see fig. 10).

[4]

fig. 10

---

[4] One student suggested that this illustration looked like a life belt and said that first you hold on to Realisation but if you start to slip you end up holding onto Personalisation and Visualisation. Finally if you were continuing to struggle you would end up clinging onto Replacement.

In summary, The Four Principles are the most vital element of The Process. Only by utilising them fully can an actor create The State of Being in such a way that they believe in the circumstances they have created. It is by using these principles that an actor can manipulate their sub-conscious.

The imagination is such a strong creative force that it needs to be used fully in order to create truthful emotions and The Four Principles are the only way to control them successfully. If you took just one idea from The Process I can only hope that it is the concept that imagination is everything and the only way to manipulate the imagination in performance is to use The Four Principles. If you do this you will become a brilliant and fearless actor.

Chapter 15
Work from the heart not the brain

"Tears come from the heart and not from the brain"
Leonardo Da Vinci

Something that I see that really can stop an actor dead in their tracks is when they start to use their brain! Acting is a visceral art that needs to be felt, there is obviously a need to use your brain when initially analysing text but that is where it should stop.

If you intellectualise you become untruthful, you stop reacting and start to pre-empt everything. You don't do this in life so why do it on screen or stage? If you start to think whilst performing, you distance yourself from your performance, it becomes clinical and precise but it doesn't live. A real case of 'Blue team itus'. I saw this the other day whilst watching a well known West End performer in a one woman musical. Her vocalisation was good but she didn't really allow her performance to come fully from her heart. The result of which was that my attention strayed from her to the use of projection, the drummer, the lighting, why the guitarist was wearing headphones and so on. The performance was technically very good but because it wasn't truthful and from the heart, it lacked the engagement it could have had. When you start to think, you start to analyse your performance and become very conscious of yourself. You allow your worst critic, you, free rein and so you will find that your performance and grasp on the truth starts to disintegrate. All of a sudden you become aware of the performance and notice what you are doing and the false nature of the performance. It then becomes impossible to create any truthful emotions so your performance becomes the worst thing possible, you are showing and not feeling. Truthful performance comes from projecting to someone. It is about the other characters on screen or stage and not about yourself. If you start to analyse and criticise yourself you will pull yourself out of the truth of the Imaginary Circumstances.

Using your brain creates a barrier between you and your emotions, it distances you from your faculties for feeling. An example of this would be if you tried to feel an emotion whilst trying to complete a complex sum. It just can't be done. Truth is a very delicate thing and it doesn't come from the left hemisphere of the brain. It is the creative, artistic hemisphere, the right, that allows you to feel and create the Imaginary Circumstances needed to produce truthful emotions in performance. So many times I have seen an actor all of a sudden stop producing truthful work or find it hard to connect with the truth of a role because they start to think. Leave your head alone when you are performing, let your heart take over. When you work from your heart you become truthful, you cannot lie if you are working from your heart. If you use your mind, that is when you start to intellectualise and interfere with your instinct. You start to think and question and complicate the situation. When you work from your heart you keep it simple and work from instinct. You can tell when you are working from your heart as it feels right, you feel connected to the character and the Imaginary Circumstances of the world you have created. When you are reacting from instinct and not censoring yourself you are operating from truth and the audience will buy your performance. Also there is nothing quite like truly performing from your heart, it is elating. You feel like you are in a real world and you react to your fellow actors with truth and create real life on screen or stage. This is what actors crave and strive for. You need to discern the difference between using your intellect and using your heart to inform your performance. The intellect is cold and logical, it is good for decision making and problem solving, but when you are performing your decisions have already been made by the playwright. Your job is to turn those predetermined decisions into impulsive and new choices. This can only be done once you have stopped using your brain and trusted in those instinctive choices that your heart will make. As an actor you should be a passionate person, if not then maybe you are in the wrong profession. Passion circumvents the brain and comes from the heart. You need to allow your passion to rule yourself. The character on screen or stage has a need and is a passionate creation, it is only fair that you engage in your passion to allow those characters to live. The heart is the soul of your character. The intellect has its role in helping to analyse the reasons your character has made the choices that it has and to ensure you truly understand what the character is actually saying and not saying (the subtext) but when all is said and done the life of the character springs from the heart. We *feel* things from the heart and intellectualise from the brain. It is essential that we *feel* the life and actions of the character.

EXAMPLE

I was playing Don John in Shakespeare's 'Much Ado about Nothing'. Don John is a very dejected character as he is the bastard son so has no real power in his family. Because of his bitterness he is always looking for a way to wreak havoc. In Act 1 Scene 3 his lackey comes to him and tries to get him to snap out of his melancholy. Don John's reaction is one of disgust as he believes that he cannot and should not change; "seek not to alter me". During this speech I had to create a sense of outrage and self pity as these are the motivating emotions for Don John. If I had intellectualised those feelings and showed them to my audience there would have been no truth. Instead I allowed my passion to rise and my heart to inform the speech. In doing so the vitriolic, anguished and spiteful nature of the character became apparent. I was operating from my heart and I felt the emotions truthfully. The result of which was that the audience really connected with Don John's feelings and although appalled by his childish reaction they felt his passion and his reasons for behaving in the manner that he does throughout the play.

Whilst we are talking about intellectualising and choosing to use your heart it is important to remember the words of Stanislavski, "On stage, put it to one side"[5]

By 'it' he is referring to using a conscious means to affect the sub-conscious. Don't consciously think about The Process whilst you are performing. All systems are for the rehearsal room and the wings, you *must BE-LEAVE* when you are on screen or stage. The danger of any system is that it can be too cerebral and that will make you detached and also question whether you are doing it right! I have, countless times, seen actors, young or experienced, start to panic if they haven't done this exercise or that exercise. When on stage they start to question themselves, thereby bringing the focus to themselves and not on their fellow performers or the world they have created. You have to get to a point where you trust in yourself, know that you have done all that you can and *Just Be*. Trust in the work you have done in the rehearsal room. If

---

[5] An Actor's work - Konstantin Stanislavski © Routledge 2008

you follow The Four Principles just before you walk on stage, you will be in The State of Being and you *will* react truthfully and instinctively. You just have to trust in yourself and your ability. If you start to think too much when you are performing, you will block yourself and in turn block any inspiration or truth, so once again....when you are performing just *BE* - and *LEAVE* yourself alone.

Chapter 16
Internalisation

"The journey of a thousand miles begins with one step."
Lao Tzu

Once you have mastered the use of The Four Principles to create truthful emotion and responses in performance you can move on the the other elements of internalisation. Unlike Stanislavski's 'System' that has a myriad of exercises that are designed to create an internal life of the character or Strasberg's 'Method' that has the actor scour the emotional past of their own life to create an approximation of truth using many other emotional triggers, The Process has distilled the important exercises to create a deeper characterisation that transcends your own personal imaginary creation. The danger of just using your imagination to create a truthful response to a character in the Imaginary Circumstances is that you can end up with performances that, although truthful, rarely result in differing characterisation. If you take Robert Duvall and Sandra Bullock you will note that their performances are incredibly truthful, they can take the audience through the journey of the character and you feel their emotion. The problem is that more often than not their performances are always the same character. They rely on the character's actions to define the character as opposed to creating an alternative reality for themselves. The downside of this approach is that you are constrained by what is written in the text, you cannot explore any alternatives. If you are playing Stan from 'Streetcar' his actions are very clear, but you are trying to fill the shoes of great actors who have stamped their individual characters on him. You cannot be Marlon Brando, you can only use your self to portray the character. If you take the text as your starting point, you can create your own Imaginary Circumstances and start to perform, but it will always be you being truthful. What you need to do is to layer on other elements to create a unique human being and explain why they react as they do to the given circumstances.

The Internalisation of a character provides further detail to the character so that it truly stands away from you as an actor and starts to have a life of its own. This also helps the actor's own belief. If you create the right internal life for your character it will remove you from yourself and help you believe in the life of the character. It also gives depth to the character. We all have a past and experiences that have formed us. Using the Internalisation exercises creates this for the character and makes it more believable.

Now, I am not expecting you to create a detailed Imaginary Past of your character from birth to the present day with all of the formative experiences and the monotony of the repeated experiences to boot. No, like using Realisation, before you start to perform, you need to find the compelling moments that are responsible for your character's choices. Like any of The Four Principles, they do not have to be in context with the character you are playing, they have to be personal to you. It is so important that you use imaginary material that could evoke the appropriate response from you.

CASE STUDY
When I was preparing for my role as Tybalt in 'Romeo and Juliet', I needed to fully understand and feel why he was so angry and full of hatred for the Montague family. I couldn't relate to some spurious slight that caused a feud as this had

no emotional effect on me. I needed something more concrete that would affect me. I decided that I would create a story for myself that would allow me genuinely to feel hatred for a third party. I imagined that the Romeo's father killed my father and raped my mother and left me an orphan. I then imagined that I had vowed to kill every member of his family as revenge. I made the time period of the event much later than the date of the setting of our production but this didn't matter. The key thing was that I had created an *Imaginary Past* for my character that affected me and helped to create truthful hatred for Romeo and all Montagues.

Creating an Imaginary Past for your character is a more creative tool than writing a dry biography of your character which is really a cerebral approach. Remember, like your Imaginary Circumstances that you create as you are working on your Realisation, you need to make it very personal and incredibly compelling, the more vivid the Imaginary Past the more emotional response you will be able to draw out of it.

Relationships
We have already explored how to discover the relationships of the characters from the text but we also need to internalise these decisions to make them real. Relationships excite an audience, they really invest in the characters if they can believe the relationship between them. Truthful relationships on screen or stage resonate with an audience and help them maintain a state of suspended disbelief. If an audience buys into the relationship on screen or stage, half of your work is done as they will believe the world that you have created and in turn believe your character's actions. Once you have them onside you job as an actor gets easier! If an audience believes in the relationships, they form an attachment with the

emotional content of the scene, again this pulls them along with you and they will be convinced that what they are witnessing is real life. Real, believable relationships create a sense of voyeurism in an audience which excites and titillates them and in turn draws them into the world of the film or play.

Relationships drive us to action. We do things because of our relationships in life, so once we have defined those relationships from the text we can explore how they affect us from the heart and so we can understand the character's actions.

EXAMPLE

For my final piece of work at Drama School, a duologue for our agent's showcase, I was performing a scene from the film "The Krays". I was playing Reggie and my partner was Reggie's girlfriend. Now it would have been easy for me to have played the stereotypical gangster and not to have considered the gentle side of the character. It was important that we defined the relationship between the two properly in order to play a real life couple. The girl I was working with was a friend and there were no romantic undertones to our relationship so we had to find something to create that spark of reality in our performance. We decided to go on a series of dates as the two characters to explore how they interacted with one another in different periods of their relationship. We started with the first date and then improvised a couple of other moments from their lives up to the time of the scene. The result of this work was that we discovered a truthful relationship between the two characters and we were specific. The girlfriend was not reacting to Reggie Kray the gangster but to Reggie Kray the boyfriend who was offering her a gift. There were some very tender moments in the scene that would have been missed if we hadn't explored the lives and relationship of the characters together. The upshot of our performance was that I managed to secure an agent which helped to start my professional career.

EXERCISE

An exercise that can help actors discover the intimacy of a physical relationship was used by the director Mike Leigh. The actors should kneel opposite each other within arms reach of each other. They should have their arms bare and close their eyes. Sensually the actors should stroke each others arms. If the actors are gentle they will feel very intimate and discover a closeness which will feed into their performance. It will also dispel the evident awkwardness that two actors usually have when they have to be intimate in performance and don't really know each other.

You won't always be able to work with like minded actors who are willing to put in the time and effort to complete such exercises, but it is important that you look at the relationship and even imagine some of the past experiences of the characters in order to flesh out your character and create truthful responses on screen or stage. The least that you should do is complete the relationship questions detailed in the Mind section of this book.

Internal Rhythm
Another tool that can be used to effect the internal life of the character is Internal Rhythm. This is developed from Stanislavski's 'Tempo Rhythm' and has a very useful application in creating depth to a character. Have you ever

been in a situation where you have had to appear calm and collected but in truth inside your heart is hammering and pounding? If for example you are in front of someone of authority and you are lying to them you would need to have a calm exterior but internally your stomach would be turning somersaults! Now you can affect your inner rhythm by truly believing in your Imaginary Circumstances, but sometimes you need something more to really engage in that sensation. The strongest stimulus you can use is music.

EXERCISE

Find a song that has the same rhythm that you feel your character has as their internal rhythm. This can obviously change from scene to scene but it is good to use this track to really inspire you so that you can key into the rhythm of your character. Once you have found a track, in a space on your own play it on repeat through headphones. Focus on the rhythm as opposed to the words and really allow it to affect you. You will start to feel your breath and heart rate change and this in turn will change your own inner rhythm. If you have chosen the right track you will find that this subtle internal rhythm will affect your performance. Once you have found the right track and allowed it to affect you, you then need to listen to the track before you perform the scene. Once you have finished rehearsals you do the same before your performance. This is a very effective way of finding the differences between you and your character and can have a major effect on your performance.

THE PROCESS

BODY

RELAXATION
LABAN EFFORTS
IMAGINARY POINTS
PHYSICAL OBJECTS
ANIMAL WORK
PHYSICAL RHYTHM
SONGS
7 LEVELS OF TENSION

6 LEVELS OF PERFORMANCE

Chapter 17
The Body

"As actors and actresses, we must rejoice in the possession of our physical facilities. We must experience joy in the use of our hands, arms, body etc. Without this appreciation and realisation of the body and its many possibilities, we cannot perform as artists"
Michael Chekov

The final element of The Process is the Body. This is the physicalisation of the character. To this point you have worked to draw the character to yourself in order to create real emotions. In Meisner's view this is enough as the character's actions, as decreed by the writer, form the character's essence. I feel that this is only half the job and an actor must discover a truthful external life for their character in order to present a fully developed three dimensional human being to an audience. To this end it is important that an actor explores all the physical avenues possible in their pursuit for a truthful character.

Relaxation
Another vital thing to be aware of in your acting and performance training is relaxation. Stanislavski noticed that when we have stage fright or are overly aware of ourselves we tense up. He saw that the best actors of his day never showed excess tension in their performance and started to develop the theory that in order to perform to your best you needed to relax and only have enough tension in your body to stand and deliver your performance.

THE PROCESS

In order to demonstrate this point, tense every muscle in your body as much as you can. Ensure that every muscle in your body is as tense as you can get it. This will take a lot of effort. Now as fast as you can I want you to solve this simple sum, what is 7 x 14? Now try and recite the colours of the rainbow and finally say the alphabet out loud backwards.

You should find that it was difficult to complete the tasks as fast as you would do so if you were not tensing so much. If being too tense can affect you completing relatively simple tasks, what effect would it have on you if you were performing?

When you have been asked to perform in class, answer questions under pressure or present to a small audience you will have discovered that you have areas of tension within your body. Most commonly these areas are the shoulders, the neck and the jaw. You could also find yourself tapping your feet a lot, jiggling your legs if you are seated or perhaps clenching your fists. All of these are symptoms of too much tension and they can have an adverse effect on your performance.

So what does it matter if you are holding too much tension whilst performing? Well as the example above has demonstrated, it makes things more difficult. You may find that you forget your lines, your moves and also your props! But that is really the lowest level of the damage that the tension is doing. The most important side effect of excess tension is that you block your emotion or emotional response to your fellow actors, this in turn means that you will not be accessing truth on screen or stage. Inspiration will only come if you are relaxed in performance. Truth and inspiration are ethereal elements of your art and are very hard to capture, so anything that gets in the way of you *being* is something that must go.

Another important reason that you need to be relaxed as a performer is that audiences are drawn to performances that are relaxed. Think back to your favourite performer, when they were in full flow, did you see them strain with veins popping out of their heads and cords showing on their necks or did they make it look like the easiest thing in the world? It is that ease that we are striving for and as such it is essential to understand when you have too much tension in your body. It is also important to understand just how much tension you need to use in order to perform. But initially we will look at how to relax and how to find tension in the body.

EXERCISE

Firstly lie on your back with your soles of your feet on the floor and knees pointing up to the ceiling. Put your hands either palms down on the front of your hips or palms up by your side. This is the semi-supine position. Just allow your back to sink into the floor, then slowly rock back and forth, side to side just to sink into the floor more. Become aware of where your body touches the floor and gently use the floor to massage your back.

Tense your feet as much as you can, really scrunch your toes and ball your feet up. Hold this for at least 5 seconds then release. Feel the soles of your feet spread out on the floor and try and increase the amount of floor you can feel through the sole of you feet.

Next tense your shins, calves and feet and hold for at least five seconds then release.
Really feel the difference between the tension and the relaxation and let your muscles feel heavy. Repeat this process from your waist down feeling the muscles that are in contact with the floor spread out and sink into the floor.
Again repeat from your shoulders down including your arms and hands, ensure you feel your back spreading out and into the floor. Finally tense every muscle in your body including your face by bringing your features into the centre of your face. Keep the final tension for at least fifteen seconds.
Once you have released all the tension in your body you should feel your body sinking into the floor. Really sense the absence of tension and survey your body for any other pockets of tension. There should only be enough to keep your knees upright.
The key part of this exercise is to really understand and feel what tension you have and release it so that you have no extraneous tension in your body. Once you can detect where the pockets of tension are and be able to release them you will be able to do this when you are under performance conditions.

You should complete this exercise regularly so that you can train your body to detect tension and then release it so that it cannot affect your performance.

How do you know how much tension you need in order to perform? There is a simple scale that you can use called The Seven Levels of Tension. This is a good way to gauge what tension level you need for different media which we will discuss later.

Once you understand which level of tension to use combined with understanding how to eradicate surplus tension, you will find that your performance will become more natural and truthful and will be correct for the different media you are performing with.

Chapter 18
Physicalisation

"The creation of the physical life is half the work on a role because, like us, a role has two natures, physical and spiritual."

Konstantin Stanislavski

So, you have worked on the truth of the character, you have strengthened your characterisation by completing the Internalisation but the character is still incomplete. You need to create a physical presence for your character otherwise you will have a very truthful version of you (remember Sandra Bullock and Robert Duval!) but not a complete character. Internalisation is an essential step in creating character but the physical life of a character gives you a real person on screen or stage.

Our life experiences are what shape us as human beings and the physical impact of these experiences can be very profound; they are part of what makes us unique. We end up carrying these experiences around with us in the form of tension and this defines who we are. Some of us carry that tension in our shoulders, some in our jaws and others exhibit it in the nervous twitching of the leg. As actors we need to harness these differences and change them in ourselves in order to create a fully rounded character. Other physical aspects of a human being that affect the quality of their movement are the Physical Rhythm at which they move and their Internal Rhythm. Different people can also have different gaits which can illustrate different characteristics. We react to people depending initially on how we perceive them; their external characteristics are the first opportunity we have to get a grip on them and decide how we will react to them. If we are approached by someone who walks with a long, strong and confident stride we are more likely to listen to their opinion than to someone who shuffles towards us with their head down looking at their shoes.

It is essential that we find actual, truthful examples of these external characteristics otherwise what we are doing is creating assumptions which lead to caricature. To this end it is important that we observe life, everything has possibilities, from the way a child unwraps and eats a sweet to the way an old man walks down the street bent double. Life is an amazing canvas on which so much rich material has been created. Stanislavski believed that art should imitate life and the only way we can hold true to this is to watch life and draw from it all the possibilities.

Part of your training as an actor requires you to train your body in order to be complete control of it. Dance, body conditioning, yoga, martial arts can all be employed to help you reach this goal. The more flexible you are the easier it is to control your body and the more aware you are of your movement the more precise you can be all this will help you to create physical truth as you explore the external elements of your character.

There are many different exercises that you can employ to help you find the external character. You can't just mimic a walk you have seen because that would not ring true in performance because it wouldn't come from you. You need to understand what physical elements affect people's physicalities as well as the psychological reasons. The exercises that we use in The Process are by no means exhaustive, but they have proven to have the clearest way to create a physical life for a character. They have been taken from Dance Practitioners, Stanislavski's 'System' and Strasberg's 'Method'.

Laban Efforts
Rudolph Laban[6] developed a method for notating dance and the classification of movements has also been attributed to his work. With the quality of a movement defined, we can develop the idea to affect a characters physical life. Laban broke movements down into three areas: Weight, Space and Time. Each of these areas have two descriptions of how they are used. Weight is either Strong or Light, Space is either Direct or Flexible and Time is either Quick or Sustained. Using these categories he defined eight separate qualities of movements which we call the Laban Efforts (see fig. 11).

Effort	Weight	Space	Time
Gliding	Light	Direct	Sustained
Floating	Light	Flexible	Sustained
Dabbing	Light	Direct	Quick
Flicking	Light	Flexible	Quick
Pressing	Strong	Direct	Sustained
Wringing	Strong	Flexible	Sustained
Punching	Strong	Direct	Quick
Slashing	Strong	Flexible	Quick

fig.11

---

[6] Rudolph Von Laban (1879-1958) pioneer of modern and contemporary dance

These efforts can be used to inform the movement of your character. Have you noticed how Tony Blair when addressing a conference uses dabbing movements with his hands and head? How about when a young teenager strops out of the room flailing their arms? Do you notice the slashing quality of the movements? I am sure you have seen someone glide into a room or wring with guilt. In rehearsal you can move around the room exploring the extreme of the Laban Effort but the key is to use it to inform the movement. There is no point in standing on stage or in front of a camera with veins popping out of your forehead because you have decided that you character's Laban effort was pressing, it's not real or truthful! You take the essence of the effort and let it affect your movement. The efforts are only one aspect of your physicality but not the only one!

Imaginary Points
As you observe people walk and move, you will start to notice that they lead with different parts of their bodies. Some people lead with their groin, others their chests and some with the top of their heads. These are their imaginary points and they can indicate a lot about their character. Those leading with their groins could be quite libidinous, those leading with their chests could be confident and those leading with the top of their head could be shy, unconfident. These are just indicators, but they can really help when trying to find the physicality of your character. Again, we start with an exaggerated representation of the imaginary points then we start to reduce it so that it only informs our physicality.

EXERCISE

Walk around the room in a circle, relax and continue to walk. Try and discover which part of your body you lead with, scan your body as you move and ascertain head, shoulders, hips, knees, feet and so on. Imagine that you are being pulled around the space by one point. Experiment leading with other points of your body and explore how that makes you feel. Try the crown of your head, then both of your shoulders. Next try leading with your chest. Note how each different point makes you feel. Note an imaginary point for your character.

Physical Objects (endowments)
Another useful tool to the actor are physical objects. This is a combination of Body *and* Heart where an actor chooses a physical object that they can endow with an emotional quality to trigger a truthful emotional response. Remember you would need to make it personal to you by using The Four Principles in order for it to ellicit a truthful reaction. For example if you are required to feel profound grief, you could could choose an everyday object but endow it with an emotional significance to you. If you have had a child you could pick a small object that your child would have had, a dummy perhaps, and then using your imagination *realise* an Imaginary Circumstance which made you feel profound grief. You could imagine that you arrived home late from work to find it burned to the ground and the only thing left of your family was this dummy. Now if you realised this fully every time you saw the dummy you would feel a profound grief that would be truthful and affect your audience.

Animal work
Animals all have distinctive movements, from the slow slither of a snake to the bounding enthusiasm of a puppy. Elements of an animal's movement can be used to help find the differences of a character's movements and your own. In drama school this technique is used by observing the animal and then recreating how the animal behaves in its own environment. This exercise is good to force the actor to really let go and stop focusing on themselves. It also is good to force the actor to drop inhibitions.

EXERCISE

Imagine an animal and really picture it in your imagination. Focus on the key elements of the animal and how we instinctively respond to them, for example the pride of a horse, the cunning of a fox, the loyalty of a dog, the disdain of a cat. How do the animals move? Are they graceful, clumsy, fast, slow? Where is their weight distributed? Is it on the tip of the toes, the heels or is it in the centre? Once this image is created, start to move around the room fifty percent animal and fifty percent human, which usually means that you are on two feet. Slowly reduce the proportion of animal to human till you are left with five percent animal and ninety five percent human. Again the point is to inform the physicality not to let it take over and make the character look false.

Physical Rhythm
As well as the Internal Rhythm, a character can be affected by their Physical Rhythm. This is to do with the character's movements. A young character will invariably move quicker whether they are walking or performing a physical action

compared to an older character. It is important that you reference this when creating the physical life of your character as it is a key element that an audience will note. If your Physical Rhythm is not congruous with the age of the character the audience will detect the inconsistency and will feel that there is something false with the performance.

As with any of these tools, you should think about them but not over think their use! All of our physical attributes are second nature, so if you put too much stead in any one of theses physical tools you will draw attention to them when you are performing and your audience will notice that something is not quite right and start to doubt the validity of your character.

A good way to help you capture the Physical Rhythm of your character is to use songs. This exercise is similar to the one used for Internal Rhythm but the emphasis is on the physical speed of the character.

Songs
The key thing to remember here is that you are trying to effect the Physical Rhythm of the character. You need to find a song that has the same physical life. Because we are not trying to affect your Internal Rhythm, it is best if you do not listen to the song but sing it yourself. In a space, walk in a circle matching your steps with the rhythm of the song you are singing. It can be any song, lets use 'The Grand Old Duke of York' as an example. Continue to sing and move, marching to the rhythm of the song until your physicality is ingrained with the speed of the song you are singing, you will invariably feel that your Internal Rhythm is being affected by this technique but the key focus should be on the Physical Rhythm you are creating. Once you feel that your *Physical Rhythm* matches that of your

song you can rehearse the scene. You will see that you will adopt the rhythm of the song in your physicality. Obviously you couldn't perform this exercise prior to every scene you are in, but if you rehearse with this enough, eventually your body will remember the rhythm you have chosen and all you will need to do during a performance is sing a couple of lines of the song to yourself to remind your body of the external rhythm of your character.

The reason you want to separate your Internal Rhythm and Physical Rhythm is because you can sometimes find that a character has conflicting rhythms. For example, if you are playing Blanche Du Bois from 'A Streetcar named Desire' in the scene when you and Stan are alone, in Scene Two, your Internal Rhythm would probably be quite fast as you are nervous and unsure around Stan as he is a dangerous and intimidating character who could brutalise you or force himself on you at any time. If you showed your fears, you would appear weak to him and put yourself at greater risk of something actually happening, also you wouldn't want Stan to see that he has an effect on you as it would diminish your status and give Stan too much confidence. In this case the Internal Rhythm would be quite fast and the Physical Rhythm would be slow to mask your true feelings. Humans operate like this all the time so it is our responsibility to create this in performance.

Energy Levels
It is paramount that you have energy to create life on screen or stage. Now this energy can be variable, but if you watch your favourite actors you will see that they have a certain vitality to their performance. This is their inner energy and they are employing the right amount in order to engage you as an

audience. Have you ever been in the room when someone walks in and they suck the energy out of the atmosphere? It is hard to be around these energy leeches as they start to have a physical effect on you and you find yourself losing motivation and the desire to achieve things. Now think about the converse situation when someone with boundless energy enters the room. How do you feel then? Do you not feel more vital and energised? Motivated to do something and do it well? I'm sure you know the answer to that question! Of course you do, energy is infectious. Other people's energy has a great effect on us in our every day lives and it plays as important a role in our lives on screen or stage.

When you have energy the audience are drawn to you. On stage in particular you can see the black hole created when an actor enters and does not have the appropriate amount of energy. It not only affects the audience, but those performing with them. They have to work harder to keep the scene alive. It is important to keep the ball in the air, so your entrance has to have the same, if not more energy, than the performers on stage. The other issue with under-energised performances is that it takes ten times more effort to revitalise a scene than it does to destroy it! If you are the one that has to come in and lift a scene, you can appear to be over acting and unreal. The balance of energy in performance is very fragile so it is your responsibility as a performer to ensure that you fulfil your obligation and bring the right amount on with you.

If you watch performers like Robert Downey Jnr. you will see that they have an uncanny ability to draw your attention. You have to watch their performances and often they eclipse their co-stars. They have a magnetism that attracts you and you can be mesmerised by their performance. Stanislavski called this

'Stage Charm', the ability to engage your audience with what seems little effort. The reason this is so is because actors like Robert Downey Jnr. have a vitality and energy that we just love to watch. His energy is perfect in the role. Enough to draw you to watch but not too much that it looks like he is working too hard! A performance needs to appear effortless otherwise you are 'performing' and the audience will see that you are 'acting' and not *being*. Energy therefore plays a great part in giving you the 'stage charm' that attracts an audience and if you are under-energised an audience will not want to watch you.

Another key reason that the correct energy is important to an actor is that without energy your performance will not reach your audience. Whether on screen or stage if you are not energised, your eyes will seem dull and your performance will not go past your nose! Stanislavski, or at least his translator Elizabeth Hapgood, coined the phrase 'radiation' when discussing how to reach your fellow actors and audience with your performance. If you employ the correct level of energy you will do just that. You will reach your fellow performers and your audience and your performance will have charm and vitality (just remember Robert Downey Jnr!).

It's all very well to go on about having the right energy levels but it is important to remember that for each different medium, a different level of external energy is required. The energy required for a performance on the Olivier stage in the National Theatre is so different from that needed when performing in front of the camera. You also need to address the amount of internal energy required regardless of the medium you need to be switched on. To this end there are two exercise that can address the internal and external energy required for performing.

The Seven Levels of Tension

This exercise focuses on the external energy needed for performance. If you remember earlier we discussed the importance of relaxation in performance and how it was key to employ the right amount of tension to keep your performance energised but also free. This exercise helps you to identify what the correct level of tension is.

EXERCISE

Walk around the room, clear your mind and keep walking, changing direction as you wish. Breathe gently and ensure that there is no excess tension in your body, making sure your shoulders aren't riding up by your ears and that your stomach is relaxed. This is your control, this is 'Neutral'. Now start to imagine that you are walking back from a relaxing day in the sun at the beach. You will notice that your level of tension has reduced and you are a little more floppy, this level is 'California'. Once you have clearly identified what that level of tension feels like return to 'Neutral' and compare the differences. Now imagine that you are on the way to an important audition, you are walking to the tube, you are on time but you have a purpose. Let this level of tension really affect you, notice your breathing and your posture, feel the energy in you rise, this level is 'Purposeful'. Again return to your control 'Neutral' and notice the differences. Now imagine that you are so relaxed that you are made of jelly, try and remove as much tension in your body whilst remaining walking. You will find that your direction will change as you walk and it is hard to control your movements. This is 'Jelly-fish'. Return again to 'Neutral' and recognise the differences again. Next I want you to imagine that there is a fire or other emergency and you are rushing to either help or get help, feel your heart rate increase and sense the urgency increase. This is the moment of fight or flight, your adrenaline starts to increase and you are ready to run! This level is called 'Emergency'. Again allow yourself to return to 'Neutral' and clock the differences. Next you need to imagine that there is a bomb about to explode in the same room and you are unable to escape. Sense the rise in your anxiety and your adrenaline. Your breath rate will increase and you will be running around as opposed to walking. This level of tension is called 'Panic'. Again return to 'Neutral' and discover the differences in the levels of tension. Finally I want you to tense every muscle in your body so much that you are unable to move. This is the maximum level of tension and is called 'Rigor Mortis', it is impossible to think and function at this level of tension. Finally return to 'Neutral' and then stop.

1. Jelly-fish
2. California
3. Neutral
4. Purposeful
5. Emergency
6. Panic
7. Rigor Mortis

These are the Seven Levels of Tension. Think for a moment and decide which is the best level for your performance.

To recap, you require different levels of tension for different mediums especially if you consider that Stage performances are like looking at life normally with your eyes, Television is like looking at life through a magnifying glass and Film is like looking at life through a microscope. We see a different level of detail in each medium. I would suggest that for Film and Television the most appropriate level of tension would be between 'Neutral' and 'Purposeful' whereas for Stage the best level would be between 'Purposeful' and 'Emergency'.

Another exercise you can use to identify the correct energy for performance focuses on the internal energy.

The Six Levels of Performance

To go hand in hand with the levels of tension, this exercise explores the internal energy that is needed to bring a performer alive on stage.

EXERCISE

Stand in the space. Clear your mind and relax. Next try and create these energy states:
1. 'Torpor' - there is no energy inside at all, you cannot be bothered to think or move or barely breathe. You feel lethargic and unmotivated and you are being sucked into the ground.
2. 'Inactive' - again your mind is blank but you are aware of yourself. You don't want to move but you could if you had to.
3. 'Meditative' - you are at peace, you are relaxed, your energy is starting to pick up but you concentrate your energy inwardly to your mind. You are starting to become alert but your energy is contained.

4. 'Active' - you start to become aware of the world outside you. Your mind is alive and you are ready to do something, engage in the outside world. Your heart rate is starting to increase and you are prepared to move. You should feel the energy building in your solar plexus readying you for action.
5. 'Performance' - you are in front of an audience. Your internal energy is starting to radiate out from you. The adrenaline is pumping and you are feeling lifted inside. You are fully engaging with the outside world and your focus is out and up.
6. 'Ritual' - You are on the summit of an Aztec pyramid about to perform a sacrifice to the Gods. This level of energy is like talking with the Gods directly. You are radiating light from your whole being and look like a sun shining your energy out, blinding the world.

Using these terms as a reference it becomes possible to identify your internal energy level and then you can then adjust it accordingly. For me a performer's energy should be somewhere between 'Performance' and 'Ritual'. Going back to our example of Robert Downey Jnr. you can feel his energy passing through the screen and see the light behind his eyes. He has the right level of energy and it is this primarily that draws us to his performances.

Chapter 19
The Next Steps

"Success is a small step taken just now"
Jonathan Mårtensson

You have looked at the text and you have explored all of the elements that make up character creation. The next thing to do is to put it all together in the rehearsal room. Be fearless, be brave and take risks! Once you have completed all the exercises detailed in this book you will have created a fully rounded and complete character based on the script. Next is to put it into practice, to rely on the work that you have done and to trust in your ability. All of the tools in this book are designed to help you elevate your performance and make it truthful. The key thing to remember is to work from your instinct and use The Four Principles to full effect. Never go on empty but don't allow The Process to get in the way of your performance. Remember once you have completed all of the background work, it is in there so you don't need to dwell on it. Just focus on your Realisation, Personalisation and Visualisation. If you are stuck you need to use Replacement but the key thing is to trust in the work you have done and don't let it get in the way of a truthful performance.

You have worked to convince your conscious mind to release your sub-conscious mind so that you will react truthfully to the imagined world that has been created. This is the route to inspiration and this is the way to ensure that you are truthful and believable.

Not everything will work for you, we all are different, but I guarantee if you use the The Four Principles and then cherry pick any other tools contained in this book that really worked for you, you will become the most truthful actor that you can be.

The Acting Coach
There is a belief in British actor training that suggests that as long as you have trained for three years you have all the skills you will ever need. Now if you think about it this is absolute baloney! How can you learn everything there is to know about acting in three scant years? I remember when I graduated from Drama School I thought that I knew everything. I put that down to youthful exuberance but what other art is there where graduates believe that? How many masters have there been who were in their twenties? It takes time and experience to actually master your art and craft. It is important that you have a belief in yourself for without this you will undoubtedly fail in our profession, but you need to realise and understand that you are always learning and any overnight success has actually worked for twenty five years to get there! Unfortunately I succumbed to the fallacy that after training I had learned everything I needed to succeed in this career. I remember one of my agents suggested that I should make sure that I went to class when I was in between jobs. I thought she was mad! The truth was that I was the one who was mad! I have learnt so much over the last ten years that I would never have learned if I had continued in that archaic mindset.

In America there is a tradition of continual development. Actors train and then sharpen their skills by attending classes as they are working professionally. They work with acting coaches on specific roles to ensure that they have as much

THE PROCESS

support as possible so that they can create truthful and believable performances. Actors attend actors' studios and are constantly developing their skills.

Why work with an acting coach? A good coach is a rock to bounce ideas off. They shouldn't tell you what to do but they should be there to listen to your ideas and then offer a different viewpoint. They should be a second opinion to the actor's choices. They need to be someone that the actor can be honest with and totally trust. Acting can be a very solitary profession with transitory relationships that shift from job to job. If the actor has one person who is a touchstone this can offer some security in a very insecure world. A good acting coach can also offer alternative stimuli in order to get the actor to find the right Realisation in order to create truthful emotions.

An acting coach can be your guide through the life of the character. They have the objective eye that can utilise the actor's emotional arsenal to help them reach the character. They are someone who will challenge the actor's easy emotional choices and this challenge will ensure that the actor is producing their best work. It takes this objective eye to highlight the easy or comfortable choices that an actor can make, choices which can make their performances samey.

A trusted acting coach can serve as the navigator through the word of the play or film. It is so easy for an actor to get swept away with the drama of the story and forsake the truthful reaction to the situation. An acting coach provides an objective eye that can be detached from the emotions of the character and the actor and therefore can find a clearer more truthful route. They have an objectivity and can see how to proceed, especially if the actor has hit a block and cannot find a way to express the emotions required by the text. The acting coach is a linchpin in an uncertain imaginary world.

Just BE!!

Everything in this book is designed to get you to create truthful emotions whilst performing. I have worked with actors using these techniques and it never ceases to amaze me to see how they develop and produce some unbelievably good work. I have seen actors and students, both experienced and those who have never acted before and who haven't been able to produce truthful work at all, suddenly transform and create the most believable, heartfelt and truthful performances all from using the simple tools provided in this book.

Take these tools, believe and commit to them, be brave, take risks and push yourself past the barriers that actors always create for themselves. If you do this I guarantee that you can become a better, more feeling, more truthful and believable actor.

Trust in The Process and you will be bright, be brave and be brilliant!

Printed in Great Britain
by Amazon